THE PORTAGE POETRY SERIES

SERIES TITLES

And the Heart Will Not Quicken
Russell Thorburn

Wildfire
Corie Rosen

Pandora's Prairie
Katherine Hoerth

How We Argue
Sharon Rose-Kourous

The Weather of Our Names
Cal Freeman

Temporary Shelters
Grant Clauser

An Introduction to Error
Deirdre Lockwood

tic tic tic
Heidi Seaborn

Lost Cathedral
Hannah Rodabaugh

Exile Is Home
Elvis Alves

Even the Sky
Kevin Thomason

The Underdream
Aiyana Masla

Dining on Salt: Four Seasons of Septets
Wayne Lee

Torrential
Jayne Marek

Users with Access: New and Selected Poems
Brandon Krieg

Flu Season
Katie Kalisz

No Trouble Staying Awake
Teresa Scollon

Another Native Tongue
Susan Riley Clarke

Catch & Release
Lauren Crawford

Steelhead
Lauren K. Carlson

The Coronation of the Ghost
Benjamin Gantcher

The Stone Tries to Understand the Hands
Susannah Sheffer

Red Camaro
Dwaine Rieves

Where Babies Come From
Ori Fienberg

Cuttings
Hannah Dow

Forgive the Animal
Sarah Pape

Love as Invasive Species
Ellen Kombiyil

They Were Horrible Cooks
Allison Whittenberg

The New Life
Wendy Wisner

Restoring Prairie
Margaret Rozga

Table with Burning Candle
Julia Paul

A Bright Wound
Sarah A. Etlinger

The Velvet Book
Rae Gouirand

Listening to Mars
Sally Ashton

Glitter City
Bonnie Jill Emanuel

The Trouble with Being a Childless Only Child
Michelle Meyer

Happy Everything
Caitlin Cowan

Dear Lo
Brady Bove

Sadness of the Apex Predator
Dion O'Reilly

Do Not Feed the Animal
Hikari Miya

The Watching Sky
Judy Brackett Crowe

Let It Be Told in a Single Breath
Russell Thorburn

The Blue Divide
Linda Nemec Foster

Lake, River, Mountain
Mark B. Hamilton

Talking Diamonds
Linda Nemec Foster

Poetic People Power
Tara Bracco (ed.)

The Green Vault Heist
David Salner

There is a Corner of Someplace Else
Camden Michael Jones

Everything Waits
Jonathan Graham

We Are Reckless
Christy Prahl

Always a Body
Molly Fuller

Bowed As If Laden With Snow
Megan Wildhood

Silent Letter
Gail Hanlon

New Wilderness
Jenifer DeBellis

Fulgurite
Catherine Kyle

The Body Is Burden and Delight
Sharon White

Bone Country
Linda Nemec Foster

Not Just the Fire
R.B. Simon

Monarch
Heather Bourbeau

The Walk to Cefalù
Lynne Viti

The Found Object Imagines a Life: New and Selected Poems
Mary Catherine Harper

Naming the Ghost
Emily Hockaday

Mourning
Dokubo Melford Goodhead

Messengers of the Gods: New and Selected Poems
Kathryn Gahl

After the 8-Ball
Colleen Alles

Careful Cartography
Devon Bohm

Broken On the Wheel
Barbara Costas-Biggs

Sparks and Disperses
Cathleen Cohen

Holding My Selves Together: New and Selected Poems
Margaret Rozga

Lost and Found Departments
Heather Dubrow

Marginal Notes
Alfonso Brezmes

The Almost-Children
Cassondra Windwalker

Meditations of a Beast
Kristine Ong Muslim

And the Heart Will Not Quicken

The poems in Russell Thorburn's *And the Heart Will Not Quicken* free enduring popular culture and literary heroes—Bob Dylan, John Lennon, Philip Levine, Federico García Lorca, among others—from their confinement each to a singular time and place. In image-rich, often intense lines, Thorburn transports them, and us, to a fresh and thought-provoking level of possibility. These are forward-looking poems, discovering the when, where, and how of what could be if only we dare imagine it.

—MARGARET ROZGA
author of *Restoring Prairie*
Wisconsin Poet Laureate, 2019–2020

I know of no living poet with a more wide-ranging fictive imagination than Russell Thorburn. His poetry is not like a novel; it's like seven or eight sometimes interconnected novels, plus a three-volume memoir. If you are new to these worlds of Thorburn, welcome! His new collection, *And the Heart Will Not Quicken*, is an ideal, inviting place to begin, knowing decades of rich narrative histories have arrived here and are also waiting when you want them. If you've been reading Thorburn for many years, you'll find in this new book the good, familiar company of old friends and meet some irresistible new ones, too.

—JONATHAN JOHNSON
author of *Pine*

And the Heart Will Not Quicken is more than a book, just as Russell Thorburn is as much myth as poet. The desolate beauty of his Upper Peninsula is inviting, not just to readers but to his heroes, musical and literary. "Lake Superior singing outside," "Motels peeled down to vacancy signs," the kind of vacancy that Thorburn haunts with Richard Manuel and John Lennon, Jim Harrison and Mallarmé. These figures all make their way to the UP to drink gallons of wine and play sets at the Old Marquette Inn because they know there's a troubadour named Russell Thorburn there to greet them, a reverent revenant, a true original.

—CAL FREEMAN
author of *The Weather of Our Names*

We never know whom we'll meet, where, and with what other literary, artistic, or historical character in Russell Thorburn's *And the Heart Will Not Quicken*. Thorburn's latest book is brimming with historical figures in a phantasmagorical landscape, either confronting their past, like the Civil War reenactor who "shows up in full costume/at the café on the highway" and "mumbles this prayer like an unstopped wound/in his throat" for the Confederate dead, or, like Philip Levine, who dreams of Walt Whitman's challenge of checkers "that day in the factory he decided he was a poet." Imagery is rich and original—Jim Harrison's "bare feet [which] stare up at him like Chinese fish" or the rattlesnake's "slither pulls on you, like D or E minor/on guitar, troubled and dark." As always, I'm drawn to our shared focus of the Civil War, the realistic and terrible human toll, as in the death of Private Orlando Metcalfe Poe, "twenty years old. . . serving with General George Custer." Thorburn brings the war into more recent ruminations about impermanence and death. Expect the unexpected when opening the pages of Thorburn's latest, rich collection.

—NANCY OWEN NELSON
author of *Five Points South: Poems from an Alabama Road Trip*

Russell Thorburn is a poet with the ear of a sixties garage band guitarist and the imagination of a magical realist whose pencil is actually a flute fashioned from driftwood washed up on the Lake Superior shore. He is equal parts Italo Calvino perched in a tree in his own invisible city and at the same time is a voice of the rural rustbelt that's Michigan-made with snow under his boots and an eye that sees the sensual in the everyday. Every poem here is a journey, a song, a myth remade in a way that only Thorburn can make us believe that everything here is true. John Lennon is still alive in these poems and is sitting at a hotel bar in Marquette waiting for you to join him. Jim Harrison too. Thorburn puts into his poems the poets who have remade him into his own instrument anew. This book is an homage to the power of such influence and how the mind can be shaped by those poets and singers we love who come before us. Enter this book to find out who next will rise up from the dead and enter your own heart. And yes, quicken it and remind you of all the ways a poem can make us feel alive.

—PETER MARKUS
author of *When Our Fathers Return to Us as Birds*

We'd all love one more song from John Lennon. It wouldn't matter if the inspiration for said song were chili or stars. It would be on my playlist as are the poems of Russ Thorburn. *And the Heart Will Not Quicken* carries Thorburn's growing literary corpus forward in—among other morsels—baseball and love poems. John Lennon is there at the Old Marquette Inn ready to sing "Imagine" on the piano. In "Baseball and Minié Balls" a Civil War soldier spills "that blue wine of his next breath" while lifting his hands above his head for a pitch that will crack like a cacophony into the catcher's mitt. With his mind on music and music on his mind, this poet knows how to hit the right note. I bet that as you read, one note in this score will work its way into you. It's worth finding out which one.

—GREG ORMSON
author of *Bears Emerge Like Stories*

Object correlative extraordinaire, Thorburn's narrative poetic suitcase opens up into multiple places, times, and cultural layers. Unearth the variegated moments in pop and literary culture: Philip Levine scrapping for courage of Whitman, Billy the Kid in the struggle before death, the milieu of John Lennon and Federico Fellini and Jim Harrison make their way into the life of stanza. This collection is his greatest because we see him not only breathe life into America, but he is everyone the line imagines who is real. The homeland of the poet, the Upper Peninsula and downstate Michigan, resonate with Whitman-esque and Thorburn-esque beauty and quill. The world he builds can only be recovered through reading the book again, which will reveal the love story of having all but nothing.

—ALEX GUBBINS
author of *To a Utopia of Graffiti and City*

And the Heart Will Not Quicken

poems

Russell Thorburn

CORNERSTONE PRESS
UNIVERSITY OF WISCONSIN-STEVENS POINT

Cornerstone Press, Stevens Point, Wisconsin 54481
Copyright © 2025 Russell Thorburn
www.uwsp.edu/cornerstone

Printed in the United States of America.

Library of Congress Control Number: 2025941889
ISBN: 978-1-968148-03-4

Cornerstone Press titles are produced in courses and internships offered by the Department of English at the University of Wisconsin–Stevens Point.

DIRECTOR & PUBLISHER
Dr. Ross K. Tangedal

EXECUTIVE EDITORS
Jeff Snowbarger, Freesia McKee

EDITORIAL DIRECTOR
Brett Hill

SENIOR EDITORS
Paige Biever, Eva Nielsen, Reilly Crous

PRESS STAFF
Brianna Loving, Leo Poskozim, Mydasia Zipperer, Sophie McPherson, Sam Bjork, Madison Schultz, Autumn Vine, Allison Lange

For my bright star, Emily, once again

CONTENTS

I.

At the Gilmore Drive-In Where James Dean
Up on the Screen Lifted His Arms Slowly   3

The Night Leonard Cohen Died   4

Deep Inside His Heart He Knows He Can't Escape
the Old Geezer He Really Is   5

Philip Levine in Detroit   6

John Lennon at the Old Marquette Inn   7

His Neck Roped in These Veins Tying Him to a Chill   8

At Big Pink Where Bob Dylan Hangs His Hat
Most of the Time   9

Wildflowers   11

Letters Jim Harrison May Never Read   12

Chagall Taught Me How to Drive   13

Walt Whitman and His Lake Superior Baptism   14

On His Sixty-First Birthday One Could See Francisco
Tadeo Isidoro Dancing in His Music Repair Shop   15

Philip Levine Dreams of Granada   16

Looking Over Woodward Avenue
at the Library Window   18

Apollinaire at Walmart   20

Miles Davis Playing on His Turntable   22

II.

All Week I Had Been Walking Down Sunset Boulevard 27

Montreal 1976   28

On Chili Night John Lennon Played a Set at the Hotel   30

Baseball Had the Blood of Many on Its Cowhide   32

When He Moved the Oars the Stars Were Tossed   33

Rattlesnake Crossing Kelbaker Road at Dusk   34

Winter's Night Bus Ride: Phantasmagoria   36

The Piano Was a Mallarmé Poem   38

D. H. Lawrence's "Coldness in Love"   39

John Lennon Rows to Dorinish   40

Bearded Oaks Made Dim Architecture   41

Philip Levine Expects Walt Whitman   42

Billy the Kid in a Phone Booth   43

Edgar Allan Poe Might Be Listening   44

Postcard from Paris   45

His Canoe over the Watery Grave of Lake Superior   47

III.

Philip Levine on His Last Poem   51

Like Any Strange Thing He Is Unsure Of   52

Julian Lennon at the Morrison Hotel Gallery,
New York City   53

Dead Man's Float   54

Beside the Breakwall near Five-Foot Splashing Waves   55

Electric Mudman Moon   56

Baseball and Minié Balls   57

The Last Tumultuous Avalanche of Light above Pines   59

A Thousand Cares Dispelled in Starlight   60

Hotel Room, Fourth Floor, Old Marquette Inn   61

Beat Poet, Beat Dog   63

My Night with Marilyn   65

Sweat Lodge   66

Kafka in Love   67

At Eighty-Two, a Shadow of Himself
Fights the Younger Leonard Cohen   68

Teaching Poetry at the Prison on Thursday Nights   69

Ferlinghetti Walking to the Caffe Trieste   70

IV.

Terminal   73

The Dream Radio's Dialed   74

Levon Helm Sings for All the Virgil Caines   75

Dead River   76

Beneath the Vulture's Slow, Circling Motion   77

He Wants the Boy in Himself to Emerge
as He No Longer Soars above His Shortcoming   78

625 Palisades Beach Road   79

Henry Zender at the Fifth Avenue Hotel   81

Entering the Classroom Benjamín Otálora   83

The Widower from Detroit   84

This Wheel on Fire   85

After Running Out of Gas on a Road
in the Mojave Desert   86

At the Séance of Mrs. Kopitzky   87

On His Sixty-First Birthday the Music Repairman
Danced a Tango while Dreaming of Cleopatra   88

One Day in May When I Opened Your Poetry   89

In Praise of My Wife on Turning Sixty-Five   90

Sergeant Reese on Leave in Athens   92

All the Cars Honking Behind Us at the Gas Station   94

A Civil War Reenactor Walks into The Mason Jar   96

The Last Photograph of Billy the Kid   98

Notes   99

Acknowledgments   107

I sing the body electric,
The armies of those I love engirth me and I engirth them,
They will not let me off till I go with them, respond to them,
And discorrupt them, and charge them full with the charge of the soul.

—Walt Whitman

I.

At the Gilmore Drive-In Where James Dean
Up on the Screen Lifted His Arms Slowly

slicked up in oil gushing from his Texas well,
Jane heard her husband crying as they sat
together in his Cadillac with its frisky finned
chrome that kept finding trees to crash.
She never rode with him when he drank.
His wife, with the model's looks of a movie star,
like Elizabeth Taylor in jeans and a southern
accent made up for Hollywood living large
in the movie with Rock Hudson, whispered
something that wasn't louder than the sound
of the earth rushing up into the air. Richard
knew he didn't have any oil well to stand under
and danced as if the whole world had changed
beneath his feet. He had lost his falsetto
for his signature song, "I Shall Be Released,"
and sank his hand deeper into popcorn
for the greasy kernels to shove into his mouth.

The drive-in theater was filled with cars
for James Dean, who never saw himself
in his film *Giant,* after he crashed into a sedan
pulling out from an intersection 28 miles east of Paso Robles.
His wife with her face full of sadness
watching James Dean, her breasts rubbing
against her braless and unbuttoned blouse,
knew this had to be the end for them.
She twirled her wedding ring round.
James Dean besmirched in the black gold
touched the whirlwind that would make
him rich, like some prophet who understood
the richer meaning of heaven lay beneath their feet.
Richard ate popcorn while sobbing. Jane opened
the busted car door to enter the drive-in night
and those gazing at the stars through their windshields,
her head not turning back for a moment, as she made
her way to the concession stand and her divorce
confessed to a friend on the payphone.

The Night Leonard Cohen Died

I was swimming with you in my dream;
your body belonged to a painting
with a fiddler floating above the town.
You were his model skinny dipping, or the cat
with a human face. Perhaps a goat tethered
to the moon. You, with your long, wet hair
and wide cheekbones, almost floating downstream
without any life, hoping to be rescued.
I did that many times for you years ago.
There was a sense as I pulled you up from beneath
the water that I would do it again.
Drowning gives you perspective or some kind
of renewed longing. I was floating through the stained
glass between your legs of another Chagall.
But you started to drown in those colors of wild
expression created by that painter. Your small breasts
pressed against my chest, closer than ever before.
Those pleasures found in the ruddy yellow earth
or the Persian blue of spires lifted toward God.
His golden voice gone to rust at age fifty,
Leonard Cohen was singing from the shore;
you might have sung back to him, his raven hair
still black and combed straight back.
He was holding the golden gun of Phil Spector,
as if he were going to shoot you full of song.
He drank the darkness, and offered a cup
to you, in the morning he would be dead.
Maybe the reason for me swimming with you,
as your body fought the darkness, and my hand
reached around your neck for a final kiss.

Deep Inside His Heart He Knows He Can't Escape the Old Geezer He Really Is

with cap and ice scraper
dancing around his frozen vehicle.
Out of luck and money, one more song
from *Bringing It All Back Home*
through his speakers.

It was "Love Minus Zero," the snowstorm
in its throes, when he climbed out
into the whirling blizzard, and knew
it was personal now,
while with the Cadillac shaking,
he stared at the bent, chrome-less fender,
not just a door swung open for the view
after varicose veins of an iced windshield
had blocked it.

He'd been driving deeper into himself,
had veered off the road into a street sign,
remembering the woman at the quarry
who turned around to look for him
after clambering up from the bank,
her hands locked into her back pockets,
Bette Davis style.

And after the jarring scrape, he thought
of her name, the woman who hurt
so much but allowed him to touch her down
at the quarry, towels over the soaking wet seats,
after they swam deeply into each other,
and came up for air, to step tenderly back
to see who truly would be standing there.

Philip Levine in Detroit

The voices outside the window are speaking
Spanish, and for a moment he dreams of Lorca
and the Guardia de Asalto executing prisoners
despite him never visiting Madrid.
He's shouting for Franny, his wife,
and he hopes he's not dead or worse.
Suddenly mad to be strapped down,
he wants to box from his toes. Throw a punch
at Sonny Liston himself, be declared
the heavyweight champion of the world.
But he's already the author of "They Feed They Lion."
He swept floors at Chevy Gear and Axle
as a young man, but wanders round the kitchen,
prying open the fridge for a beer. It has to be a Stroh's,
and when he peeks down between his legs
after shadowboxing the form growing larger
every minute against the kitchen's dull yellow wall,
he recognizes his old friend hanging there
between his balls. He calls out to his shadow,
but shakes his head and sees his cock swinging.
He breathes heavily although he hasn't had a Lucky
Strike in twenty years. His heart is exhausted
from boxing, feinting with one extended jab,
following up with an uppercut. In another dream,
Walt Whitman challenges him to a game of checkers
that day at the factory he decided he was a poet,
feeling deep into his pocket for a poem he wrote
for the long hours of waiting in line for work.
They're drinking beer at a table outside
when Levine hears his heart rushing forward,
like the night swimming in the Detroit River
with a Polish girl, but he can't remember
her name, only her bare thighs wading into the brine
that would always be a baptism for some.
Whitman in his forest of hair studying him
as he removes the wooden pieces from the board.
When he hears the automatic go off he is too
dead to know that he has never been to Madrid.

John Lennon at the Old Marquette Inn

Last night he was talking to Federico Fellini
in the bar on chili night, who told him, "I'm not afraid
anymore of telling the truth." John Lennon was celebrating
his 84th birthday, as if the years no longer mattered.
He wanted his whiskey. Like Jim Harrison, I said,
who wasn't actually dead like everyone else.
His poems scared all the birds from his head.
"Fear makes for good servants."

His body spun on his stool and the Liverpool boy
talked about Lake Superior singing outside.
Angry waves exploded in his chords
on a Gibson he had left out all night in my car.
It had an ugly sound that suited his darker edge.
His wire-rims were replaced by designer shades now,
all his shirts made in Rome. He cursed when his tie
dove into a chili bowl and stained his Piero Gherardi suit.

When Fellini had told Lennon about his wife in bed,
his eyes opened wide, ready for outer space.
John slept alone with the television on.
Some nights he asked me to join him. We read
Harrison's poetry of birds and rivulets
flowing between a woman's legs
on her walk through Mulligan Creek.

John Lennon suddenly splashed on some trousers
and explained he was going to knock on Fellini's door.
The Beatle standing alone on the fourth floor
would catch my nineteen-year-old girl walking to the bathroom.
She would smile at him just when we happened to see
Jim Harrison with his manual typewriter
telling us he was going to write a novel on the hotel roof.
The ingredients were the stars, he told Lennon,
as if he wanted one more song from him
to sing of a woman's body bathing in a stream.

His Neck Roped in These Veins
Tying Him to a Chill

He steers the canoe toward shelter, the ice-crusted
beach where a few trees stand solitary. Letting go
of the paddle, the Union soldier drifts through
the bared teeth of the whitecaps. Above him stretches
the bruise of a snowstorm; the first snowflakes
are flying away like his heart. His puffed knuckles
stab at his mouth with a cigarette to ward off the chill.
He touches his almost forgotten color of blue on his tunic,
fingers thinking through the hanging buttons.

What happened to his girl, the one with blue eyes
unable to cry when he joined up with General Custer?
Her body would not wait for him, she would give herself
to young men. When he walked away into snow
he heard her shout for him to die. He thinks of the cold
as an angry woman; snow whirls around his shoulders
in the shape of her breasts, her belly this bowl
of enormous cold white flesh, and this great pain twists
his intestines as his canoe chops through the rolling waves.
He should have died at Shiloh, and his twenty-
something body buried under loose stones.

Muskets, every living lead ball, plucked like plenty
from his still arms that day when countless others
lay unnamed in their graves. Let me be released,
the young man with frost lines under his mottled eyelids
intones to the weather. His canoe bucking toward
the museum of a frozen shore with its trees bending
in the heavy ice and those marbled statues alive.
Their limbs strangely beckon to him, but
his brown eyes like old shoes want to walk away.

At Big Pink Where Bob Dylan
Hangs His Hat Most of the Time

Some say there was nothing on that road
but a rock star who wanted to climb down
from fame for a while, rest in country shade after crashing
his motorcycle on Striebel Road; nothing for him
but to hide behind a farmer strolling
through his sun-kissed crop of hay.
He believed his motorcycle on its own volition
could chase him down to his old dusty manual
that left him to squint at nicotine keys.

The avocado-colored phone off in the kitchen
and the Formica table covered with coffee cups,
mostly empty, along with cigarette packs,
next to sheets of scribbled lyrics. Bobby tore back
the manual carriage after completing a phrase
to match Richard Manuel's melody for "Tears of Rage,"
and stared at it, as if he didn't know what was next.

His beautiful wife Sara, once a stripper in a club
who caught the eye of that short fellow
from Dinkytown, kept calling every hour,
wondering when he would be coming home
for dinner. Still recording at Big Pink,
he straddled the basement steps for the Tapes
he hoped would hit vinyl; or something
on the softly cracked subterranean style
of "Yazoo Street Scandal" nobody
would bother to breathe into a microphone.

Dylan at the typewriter, his cigarette ember
his burning third eye of a prophet, was ready
to see something on par with lightning striking a giant oak.
Richard Manuel watched him as he stood up
slowly from his chair, all the words written today

assaulting him one more time. Bobby saw it clearly,
darker than the crows on the clothesline,

out of the corner of his eye, that fame
which toppled his motorcycle, the harvest
whose weight he couldn't bear as a folk singer
or rock and roll messiah for a generation
he didn't want a thing to do with.

The prophet lit a cigarette to take
down wherever they were going in song,
hoping there was a way to return as normal men
who could rock in chairs on the porch
and talk about growing old.

Wildflowers

Everything beautiful dies eventually,
he whispers as if writing it into a poem,
but the wound-dresser from Long Island
strikes his heart from his own pain.
A blessing issues from his lips,
a kind of Kaddish, when he kisses
him on the cheek and straightens.
When he walks to the clear creek
where the crows call out for the flesh
of berries, his stained shirt falls
into broken grass sweetly growing.
The nurse who followed him
wades into the water before him.
Her face appears younger
when she trembles from the cold,
and the poet sees her staring over
at his half-naked aging body.
Her name eludes him somehow,
but he thinks it's Agnes when she laughs
at herself lifting up her blouse,
washing her exhausted skin.
In the distance a cannon can be heard,
the earth swallowing men, a sharpshooter
who takes aim from high up in a tree.
All day the nurse and Walt Whitman
have tended soldiers who have fallen,
wounds now purple with gangrene.
Dear comrades, some cry, if they are able,
or can see, you will be joining us soon.
The silent creek is himself, he whispers
as names float through the air, unable
to speak of the dead flowing under
him that are caressing his legs, like the wind
that will meet the hungry stars above.

Letters Jim Harrison May Never Read

He walks barefoot through the snow
and doesn't let the cold bother him
as he unlatches his mailbox. He rubs his bare
head with a hand he has just discovered is real.
The days are full of characters who are divers
for the Grand Marais Salvage Corporation or are known
as Brown Dog. His simple mission is to collect
the growing mail: the large yellow envelopes
from Boulevard Saint-Germain piling up on the ground
from the poets back in Paris he once shared
a 37-course meal at a restaurant in Saint-Père-sous-Vézelay.
They were cooked using culinary guides published between
1654 and 1823, in Spanish and French; and they ate
while reciting Jean-Paul Sartre's *Being and Nothingness*,
as if his words were only a kind of early dessert.
His bare feet stare up at him like Chinese fish,
starting to turn purple in the winter light.
He wants to collect his mail and return inside
to Ethiopian coffee before he considers anything more,
like Rimbaud and his slave trade in the heart of Africa.
When he sees a letter in a small, crumpled envelope, he wonders
if it's the woman from Arkansas again, her body
forever on his mind after she sent candid photos of herself
leaning over her palomino without any clothes on.
He was conscious of her nipples pressed against
horseflesh with flies buzzing around her ass.
Then there was a letter he wrote himself to see if he'd answer,
as if there was no other way to question existence.
Unless it was a pinball machine in Paris,
or some café in Casper, Wyoming that never gave a shit
if he drank all day without wearing trousers
or made sure the cook roasted enough pigs to persuade
the entire town to eat themselves before the sun sank.

Chagall Taught Me How to Drive

Through the rumble of a borrowed Chevy,
we waited for her baby to be born,
our nights sliding under the tires like a Chagall
painting of the wedding couple floating above town.
The beautiful breasts of my girlfriend
like frosting on a wedding cake. She steered me
blindly across the road with one hand,
avoiding a levitating fiddler, Chagall himself
standing on the side of the road, showing us
he had seven fingers to paint faster.
My girlfriend was pregnant, and she taught me
how to drive, her cheekbones pressed against my shoulder.
When I strayed out of my lane, she said to keep left,
pretending the faded white line was a child.
I hadn't fathered the road or the baby inside her.
Nor would we ever float loose above wooden fences,
pass through a window into Paris.
She didn't want to birth her baby alone:
her belly barely fit behind the steering wheel.
I drove thirty miles per hour, slowing down
for peasants who were dancing in the road,
thinking they must be from Belarus, where
Chagall first painted on stained glass:
these ghosts from his past now stared at us.
We were headed for the beach in our borrowed Chevy.
The trees waited for us to find them human,
as they stood one after another, with their arms raised.
I counted them along the road until one bent in heartache,
and this was where we turned off for the shore.

Walt Whitman and His Lake Superior Baptism

Memory mixes in with the first chill of the water.
He looks upon that blue of Lake Superior
like a mother's apron, and uses its clarity
to cleanse himself, direct his hand to point
toward a ledge of rock named Ripley.
The Civil War remains behind him with
his rucksack of journals, the words stripped.
Whitman peers down at his toes moving
over the sand underwater, its mirror
reflects his overweight body.
He fits his belly into this baptism,
allowing the cold to touch his knees, bruised
hips next, forcing his living breath
to meet the waves with his watery kiss.

On His Sixty-First Birthday One Could See Francisco Tadeo Isidoro Dancing in His Music Repair Shop

Francisco danced a tango to the vinyl record
of an Iraqi orchestra, not caring he turned sixty-one
and the cigarette in his hand would probably
kill him; he was going to celebrate the cobwebs
he brushed away from his past in his repair shop.
His whiskey he made himself in his backyard shed,
sipping the minutes like a clock that tasted of charcoal,
all those honeyed ingredients that he poured in later,
like words from the blind fictionist named Borges.
The irregular troops beating their way north
to join the divisions under the command of Lopez.
Francisco, taking off his shirt, looked down
on his bouncing belly and his Excelsior accordion
like a snowy owl who had flown in from a window.
He boldly kicked out one foot, then the other,
not caring he was sixty-one today; in his repair shop
he smelled of cigarette smoke and whiskey drunk.
But the police detective, Mendez, had come again
to inquire about his missing wife, Patricia,
who was accused of murdering a policeman,
for that animal had assaulted her sister.
In those tremulous depths of his birthday,
the secret was lurking, so he began strumming
a classical guitar with Willie Nelson's autograph
on the pickguard. Francisco was sure Mendez
never read Borges, and he felt bendable as catgut
when he matched a tune to his own destiny.
A dead man from the labyrinth of Mexico City,
what did his name matter when Mendez
aimed his cold barrel at the musician? But he told
him anyway, if you are going to kill me, please
regard the corpse as one Francisco Tadeo Isidoro.
And know today it is my birthday, and pour
yourself a whiskey to help me pass over
the rooflines and inexhaustible repetitions
of every man's confusion on this heavenly day.

Philip Levine Dreams of Granada

Sleep takes him to the unexpected snow
on Grand River Avenue, the massive streets
with their French façades of some city
he can't ever reclaim, but now dream voices
are speaking Spanish, and for a moment
he's digging his own grave beside Lorca.
"Federico," he's saying, "what's it like
to be dead?" The Spanish poet with his hair
slicked back like a matinée idol laughs.
The Guardia de Asalto watch them,
not expecting snow on Grand River Avenue,
or how dreams can change their channels
like television, and Philip Levine
tells Federico to have a seat in his apartment
in Fresno, California. "We will go outside
and pick some oranges. Eat each one
and compare their succulent flesh
to the last woman whose bed we shared."
Federico, his shirt unbuttoned to show
his chest is sweaty, follows the Detroit poet
to the orange tree in his front yard,
its dark branches laden with oranges.
The Spaniard bites into a juicy one,
and talks about a woman with thick legs
that he once swam a river with.
They don't expect the Guardia de Asalto
to come walking out of his television.
Philip lights a cigarette secretly,
hoping his Franny won't smell the smoke.
He mixes another Manhattan, and hears
the Saturday night fight crowd shouting
over the verdict. Sonny Liston demanding
his corner retrieve the towel thrown in during
the seventh round with Muhammad Ali.
"I am not going to lose," he mumbles.

Philip wants to rise from bed,
but can't swing his legs off the edge.
Punch drunk, he sees Muhammad Ali
swinging that meaty fist over Liston.
All those enemies calling for the earth
to be totally theirs and not anyone else's.

Looking Over Woodward Avenue
at the Library Window

Seated in the frayed upholstered chair,
I often wondered if my death would come
from reading a Russian novel by Dostoevsky,
missing the bus that would take me home
from these mountains of good books.
Not in a khaki army uniform in a jungle,
wire-rims coated in a tiny sea of sweat
and helicopters screaming overhead.
I planned to read *War and Peace* next week,
if I ever finished *The Idiot*, and that could
be a lifetime of reading and sitting comfortably
in someone else's life, like Myshkin's, taking
the bus each day downtown to Detroit
for more fat books of fiction, at least a pound
or two, the pages coming undone from
a false stitchery, and my ankle-length hiking shoes
making my feet sweat as if they were already in Vietnam.
I looked through a large window at hours
slowly turning toward bamboo fields that now
felt close with the Tet Offensive on TV every night,
an M-16 in my arms as I lay flat and helmeted
and too young to know I was going to die.
I wouldn't read Levine's poem,"On the Murder
of Lieutenant José del Castillo by the Falangist
Bravo Martinez" until much later despite
riding buses around Detroit without a future.
I returned each book to the library shelf,
knowing today wasn't my dying day
and that would make my mother glad
I'd be home before eleven to watch
the evening news with her. Look at the gone
world that explodes into an evening's dark.
One day I'd start growing my hair
and every morning I knew I could always

go back where I came from, walk to my local
library for a book by Robert Heinlein
called *Stranger in a Strange Land*.
To love another person. To finally grok
was what I wanted as that young man
in corduroy trousers and wire-rims,
tousled brown hair. My mother made sure
I always left home with seven dollars,
seven for luck, I guess, as if she never
expected to see me again and seven dollars
would keep me alive if I got drafted one day.
Out of Catholic high and going nowhere.

Apollinaire at Walmart

For David Dodd Lee

The bandaged poet nudges his cart down the aisle,
his legs slightly bowed when he stands
at attention before a mirror, with that curious
root between his legs aroused at seeing himself alive.
So many of his friends are dead, and defying
any store policy, he lights up a Russian
cigarette he had been saving to smoke
after riding away from his trench with the artillery.
Ah, he appears to breathe, his shoulders trembling,
as if he were a fallen star that still explodes.
His loves are those memories dug out of his hypogeum.
Those Russian temptresses like Akhmatova
who slept with many poets before she married.
But his cart almost veers off into a display
of jars full of salsa labeled red hot.
His overweight body slipshods onward
like the wildest of villanelles that crash
across the disinfected floor. The Russian poet's
visible moon still on his mind until a pretty cashier
wearing hoops for earrings yells, "You can't smoke
in the store," and still bleeding from barbed wire,
he flicks the butt at the rest of the world.
He's wearing a blue steel helmet called an Adrian.
The large pockets of his great coat contain
shrapnel like metal fragments of his poetry.
Only human skin protected himself from the Boche,
and producing an orange like a grenade,
his teeth set off an explosion of this citrus
from the family of Rutaceae. Like a Picasso
breast depicted on one of his canvases,
Apollinaire thinks of Galileo and a round earth.
How the human body provides this roundness
and certain holes of existential pleasure.
He delights in these shapes of sexual geometry,

like Pablo attempting to connect the missing bodies
of these women who will come into existence.
Pushing his cart forward, Guillaume shudders
at the tender cry of an announcement,
then realizes neon lights recognize the eternal,
as he heads for the door with his empty cart.

Miles Davis Playing on His Turntable

Reese scraped back his folding chair from the table,
his feet lost in these steps waltzing
him barefoot across the cold floor. His turntable
was playing a record of Miles Davis,
its needle igniting his loneliness
again on this lonely night in Paris. America
so far away from him, like his jacket with
soft pink pockets full of postcards never mailed to
family who were all strangers now
in those places he could never call home.

They were shooting people at the Bataclan,
and he looked for his old shoes as he bent
down to reach under the table filled with dinner plates
and a bottle of Bordeaux
only half drunk–to hell with socks,
he decided, thinking of his grandson who wrote him letters,
crooked block words, a blockhead sergeant
who boxed for bloodlust, but good-hearted too.
Up on his ledge he kept a photo of him,
to remind his aging heart that he had kin.

If he thought more than two minutes about it,
but he never did that now after his seventieth birthday—
a man who vowed to never return home
after Germany surrendered, a decision made in Munich
of all places, where he had reposed
in Hitler's bathtub with the *Vogue* journalist,
Lee Miller, both of them wearing only their steel helmets,
and he should have kissed her when he had the chance
before she poured the tub full of steaming hot water.

Leaving the kitchen table to fight, spilling a splash
of bitter Ethiopian coffee he drank every day,
he slipped on his goddamn shoes, no socks necessary

as he hung his wire-rims around
those radar station ears and checked his Glock
to see if it was loaded. Full fucking clip, and down the stairs
like a crazy man, swinging his arms around like haymakers
in the Tenth Arrondissement, he imagined the cordite smell.

He'd fire high at the head of the first bastard,
then low into the gut, if he wasn't shot himself,
but at seventy he'd take his chances, and let his grandson's
letters pile up like slightly read newspapers—
he wrote about boxing, battering a man's face
called Sugar Baby—and Reese closed his eyes
and was back at the farm, with the wind in his hair
threading together his wife pregnant with a son he'd never meet.
His grandson told him in one of the letters
his father made an art of drawing naked women.

He got well paid for them, many of them used
for illustrations in novels or magazines—
and he had sent one for his grandfather
to size up and the only thing he saw was a coward
who never joined up unlike his son who had fought in Fallujah.
For a minute he was twenty years old, and considered
a short burst into a policeman's bulletproof vest
who told him to stop walking toward him—his Glock
was concealed in his open shirt, and his heart,
with a hole in it, soon juddered, and he fell hard,

his wire-rims flying off, and if he didn't see
her hands he felt them grasping his,
her name Monique, she whispered sweetly,
despite people being killed—
and he beheld her blonde blur helping him
stand up—he'd stagger all the way back
to his apartment, almost crying, not for her as much
as himself, alone again, and without family, his glasses
not found, as he hated this life suddenly
holding his gun close to his heart.

II.

All Week I Had Been Walking Down
Sunset Boulevard

My body on fire, twisting to the truth
of nothing left to lose, wanting to return
with a poem that wouldn't be a lie.
Johnny Cash matched my mood; it would
only take a minute to turn back the clock.
But on New Year's Eve, Johnny's gospel voice
washed away my sins on Sunset Boulevard.
"Ring of Fire" blasted from the coffee shop's stereo,
and the baristas cleaned off the tables
of these spilled dreams and Styrofoam.
I fell into his burning ring of fire. How the flames
went higher because June Carter loved
a married man. She gifted Johnny that song.
I only felt like I was cheating as long
as that song was bound by desire.
My favorite barista was named Bathsheba;
her silver hoop earrings dangled from her lobes.
"You know, you're very attractive," I told her.
She handed me my cardboard tray of coffees.
"Love is a burning thing," the man in black sang,
and my pen would tell the truth of no money
for a middle-aged poet in the heat wearing an Irish cap
who circled back to his marriage, for Johnny's
song was sending me back down to be born again
despite the barista and her eyes like blooms of fire.

Montreal 1976

Notice I am drunk and lost on the subway,
the twenty-four-year old me unsteady
on my feet, watching for the wrong turns,

but my girlfriend and her daughter
are waiting back at our tourist room.
My hair a slow-moving current

and eyes fish swimming, ahead of me
is a strange dream of Ste. Catherine—
and I can't tell my lover I was lost.

Or why Carlos got back first at the hotel
despite buying all the drinks and attempting
a kind of French to pick up barmaids

at a topless bar—and pissing in the lavatory,
my own French flopped forward like a lazy
hound when addressing a fellow drunk.

At a diner I eat a scrambled egg sandwich,
hoping for sobriety. Nothing happens.
Every street wrong, the right ones

in another language. Nobody came back
to the tourist rooms with Chinese take-out—
on our last night in Montreal, Carlos's

wife, a stripper who once performed
with her wedding lace on, was waiting
for him to say why. Montreal appears

to be a flesh pool with everyone
walking around, splashing through
those puddles of desire.

See me walking stunned, farther
from the strip club on Ste. Catherine,
where a long-legged girl strips to Joe Cocker

singing "You are so beautiful," and she
was, dropping to her knees and lifting
her hands up in this prayer for her body.

Her nipples untranslated code as she bent
her torso in half, rising from the floor.
Notice me, twenty-four years old,

another face in the crowd.
My girlfriend back at the tourist room—
on our last night in Montreal.

The night I lost myself on the subway.
My mind can't contain any of this,
so that's why, reader, you are with me,

in this splendor of a garden, consider
it must be Eden, drunkenly so.
But I couldn't breathe a word, stumbling

toward my girl, who was upset too,
her eyes burning, as she looked away.
Picture me, talking without saying

where I've been tonight.
Carlos pulls me aside and whispers,
"What are you going to say?"

On Chili Night John Lennon
Played a Set at the Hotel

John Lennon wasn't going to start a set in the bar
without drinking his vodka. The living grew closer
as he spun on his stool, and at the hotel
where he was staying for an eternity, he spooned
the last of his chili to his Liverpudlian lips,
and told the crowd of bartender and several housemaids,
this was the only way he could feel alive.

A microphone and a small amp at the front
of the bar, he entered that Beatle world with "All My Loving,"
strumming madly that familiar riff.
He didn't mind there were no girls screaming
their sexual frustration, no security guards
grabbing their thirteen-year old arms
while they rushed the stage. He peered back
in sunglasses that Marcello Mastroianni wore in movies,
and straddled wide his spot of fame
wearing form-fitted black trousers.

"I am just a shadow of a frazzled hyperreality,"
the ex-Beatle thought while the lyrics kissed his mouth,
in this Dickensian universe full of locked rooms
he was forever escaping, and he leaned his head
out the open window for a moment
to feast on wind and snow.

He believed in wild girls and gallons of wine,
and it wasn't clear by morning if he had slept.
He rang room service to hear another voice
that told him he was human. He scribbled lyrics
for May Pang in the bathroom, an overwhelming
delirium that traveled across the hotel stationery's small pages,
composed while looking out at Lake Superior.

When he broke a string, he asked the bar mirror
if he had aged with his hair starting to gray,
expecting no answer back from the glass.
The piano bench was where he sat to play out his set,
loading the next song in his head, lifting it up
for the powerful sense of a lost childhood.
"You say I am a dreamer, but I'm not the only one."

Baseball Had the Blood of Many on Its Cowhide
March 25, 1870

The farmer heard the sound of a bat tearing at the cowhide.
One fielder had only one arm who scooped up the path
of the ball's trajectory, unsheathed his cornsack glove
with no fingers, and took that delicate egg in his remaining hand.
These killers played a sport in the sunlight's yellow and a wind
that smelled of gangrene. There was a suicide squeeze walking
the line of dust, and the long-legged boy on third base ran home.
The farmer knew his father, who had lost both legs a year ago.
If he squinted into the sun, he could see him perched in a chair
out past his potato patch. The blood of many was rubbed
into the cowhide. The burnt crops harvested only ashes
that year, and each bone tasted of sons who never made it home.
Sometimes he saw Robert E. Lee rubbing up cowhide,
but he had to wipe away the grit from the dust blowing
away their way of life. When he looked twice there was only
a one-armed hurler who bent for dirt to spin a curve,
like the sun going down behind the moon in an eclipse.
He would leave his bed, creaking floorboards in a sort of mercy,
his wife eight years younger ignoring his body,
as he wound a sheet around himself to stand in the field.
His heart tried to keep up, but it let him go like an idiot,
holding out his arms in the blistered starlight
before he outran the sound of his angry breath.

When He Moved the Oars the Stars Were Tossed

Just enough to drift deeper into the bay
where the quiet was fireflies and families shouting
from the shore, his bare feet looked up
at him from the bottom of the rowboat,
toes wiggling forlorn in the warm water.

If the stars mattered, they were tossed
into the air, that bowl of night turned
upside down; and they frightened him
if he didn't breathe, tilt his head
of longish-brown hair up to the sky.

His worn hands on the oars shifted
to break the mirror of the water
that distorted these silhouettes beneath
branches and leaves; underwater grass
waving luxuriant in the moonlight.

Let moonlight be seen through a milk bottle,
shining upon his body, but his words
echoed without response, and releasing
his grip from the oars, he knew winter
was coming closer each time he rowed.

The oars dripped onto the mirrored
water of his sixteen-year-old self,
and as he fathered himself, he wanted to swim
beside the rowboat, asking the current
to pull him along the shore.

The first bullfrog burped from the cattails
like a mud song for the moon, the mosquitoes sang
around his head, biting his earlobes,
and he wondered if he'd see a shooting star
as the music of the oars followed him home.

Rattlesnake Crossing Kelbaker Road at Dusk

That slither pulls on you, like D to E minor
on guitar, troubled and dark,
syncing with a blood-red moon,
but you're a good judge of darkness,
having seen it when you were nineteen
on the coastal highway to Berkeley,
writing this poem inside your head,

moving over the earth, flying like a hawk
over desert sand. You see nineteen on this road.
The mountains talk to you like they always do,
about sleeping at a garbage dump,
longing to fall in love. How the last rattle
of the snake coils at a freight train among
the sand-brushed cholla cactus,

and if you leave the car watch for coyotes
with their tongues hanging out.
There's a river of sand, and that fading
hallelujah of an earth
that never leaves you alone.
You recall the abandoned house where you slept
before the police arrested everyone,

but you weren't there that night. You had business
elsewhere, like a rebel without a cause.
Let me not waste time on impossible flights,
nor scatter my strength
in self-pity and fear of hitchhiking
across the Golden Gate. But those words are sprinkled
over the sand like stardust.

If you wander from the star-crossed headlights
that mark where your car pulled off Kelbaker Road,
walk over the rattlesnake burrows in prayer

for those who've vanished. That's yourself
wearing those big black glasses. Look at a shooting star
for evidence of being nineteen again–you're out there
like a meal for the hungry.

Winter's Night Bus Ride: Phantasmagoria

The late hour of a boy looking for himself
in the reflection of a bus window as he travels
back through his heart at three a.m.
Even upon arrival the boy and his lover will be alone.
He wonders if she's asleep now,
and what his lover will say when he arrives.
Or why Tim Buckley died so young
last June in LA, and he pondered Vietnam
and nearly being drafted, body bags
coming home on TV, but Buckley overdosed
before he could record another album.

Instead of lurching on this lunatic bus,
he wishes he could bury his beating heart
against her belly in that large feather bed,
clear this dream to its pure slumber.
He'd tangle in her breath instead
of the breath of a man, also lunging
three seats behind him, slouched forward,
cut in half by a hallucination, perhaps.

It is the nightmare man with bird-like eyes,
a coat wrapped tight around a raven's neck,
all gristle and bone and ready to be snapped,
who mumbles words of a drug addict,
a stand-in for Tim Buckley from LA
aboard a Greyhound knocking through the Upper
Peninsula, and who disturbs this young dreamer
watching a deer gaze at the apparition
of a bus sunk into wintry depths.

Snow scrapes the windshield faster
than the wipers can clear this wedding of trees
standing knee deep in the snow,
waiting for the morning to arrive.

The bus driver cranes his neck
toward the shadows, shuffles the door open
to yell at a surprised fox with an unraveled tail,
ravens squawking, who have wandered
into his headlights. He yells, the cold
ghosting in with the miles.

The boy hears the Tim Buckley stand-in
talking nonstop black jagged shadows
reminding him of doom, and he watches
his own face in the bus window
trying to read his bearded reflection.

A woman with gray hair, beautiful in her own desire,
sits across the aisle from him at the end
of a cigarette. She's as thin as her Lucky Strikes,
and speaks to him ardently about nothing:
maybe the snow levels or the farms
they're passing, her eyes full of some
longing for a destination only she knows.

His wire-rims chafe his nose, a finger pushing
them back, they're always pinching him,
and he sees the moon sawed in half,
but closes his eyes, uneasy about sleep
because of the sad-looking barns with weathered veins,
motels peeled down to vacancy signs,
all the yellow lines we cross over in our dreams.

The Piano Was a Mallarmé Poem

One that couldn't be translated but looked up
at you with its broken mouth, teeth
still grinning and black flesh that trembled
when you touched and made a wrong chord.
On your piano bench you leaned in
to find the proper melody, your elbows out
as if to catch the stars that were falling
and that blood moon unwavering above
when you couldn't find the right notes.

You heard your mother in the kitchen,
as if she had much to do with your artlessness,
her smoking an afternoon cigarette
while making lunch for you, her darling boy
without a job who lived in the basement.
In the kitchen was her Mallarmé,
there in the pots and pans, the washing
of silverware until they shined, as if she understood
Poe's saying that the French gave
"a purer meaning to the words of the tribe."

The piano wasn't tuned in years,
but was never forgotten where it rested
beside your mother's sewing machine,
an upright grand your grandmother
let loose in ragtime, catching
her youth with that Scott Joplin tune.
You held court with the soft pedals,
mesmerized by the hammers
striking the architecture of the harp
with its steel strings and so many notes
you sent stumbling around you,
as if you couldn't translate
what you knew was in your soul.

D. H. Lawrence's "Coldness in Love"

He throws back an apple as an afterthought,
one bite taken out of Eden, his fortune
found unread in the grounds of his coffee cup.
Something about marriage, he contemplates,
hearing his wife murder a chair at the table
when she settles her large, merciless hips.
He bends as close as he can to the morning scraps;
almost on the tips of his toes, his eyes
like hummingbirds racing along avenues
where time hasn't begun on the unlined spaces.
Let the sun be enormous in your heart,
he wants to say, as if he can't escape it.
An empty cup of coffee fills his tongue
with leftover grounds, and he doesn't have
the steam to rise from his chair for more.
Every day has led him to believe in silence,
as if his Midland ears were born to listen
to his wife and her roundness disturb
the order in their Taormina villa.
She stands up to sunbathe, nude and rattling
her chair legs across the stone floor.
Outside he will peek at her beautiful loins
as she scares the black flies buzzing around her belly.
His pencil appears inadequate to scrawl another
word onto the landscape of an empty page.
Best to abandon it while he can, unable to praise
her ass when she bends down for her sun hat
that has tumbled from her crown of frizzy hair.
When she sits herself on a rickety kind of bench
to sort through her letters that came from Metz,
a coldness will return to Lawrence. He lights
a cigarette, pondering her sunburned shoulders,
head bent at someone else's feast of words.
His shirtsleeves rolled up reveal his white skin,
never naked in the sun, and when he seats himself
comfortably beside her, he will write a cramped
cursive of how the loveless can never love.

John Lennon Rows to Dorinish

He has bought an island out of his fame
to hide away in years approaching forty.
That nose down in the wind,
his septum trouble from too much
of everything, his brown hair curling
from under his Spaniard's hat with a string,
his ears like large question marks he can't deny,
"why am I rowing like an escaped convict
to this Irish island?" his cheeks aflame
from the raw touch of the wind's lashing.

All I want is to get to my Dorinish,
he murmurs like a ghost swooping from ashen sky,
lifting him almost out of the rowboat
he had to buy for too much money.
He's got blisters on his fingers, and the splash
of strident waves against his weathered prow
demonstrates he is moving toward that lump
barely visible in the water. They told him
he'd have no difficulty with the oars
and the mile or so to row, but he knew
his son would never visit him here.

His blisters are bleeding and he hates
this sea he's on, the gunwale leaking water,
so cold on his Italian boots. He beholds
his bell bottoms soaked and clinging
to his ankles—a skirl of sun
over this next part of nothing,
rowing himself for a home.

Bearded Oaks Made Dim Architecture

Decay always descended, so he turned back home
and creaked floorboards in a sort of mercy
to his marital bed where his younger wife
waited for him. He stretched out in bed,
still young enough to want to devour her.
He raised her nightgown up above her belly,
shouting as the evening curtains billowed.
He would never walk the earth again,
like he had before, and the moon had risen
over the ashes of his field. He wanted to hurry
away in defeat, but first he would arrange
her body from behind and fill her up with gold.
The stars began to swim down to earth.
He heard cannons fired up toward the treeline
that severed the sun, and they fought without
ammunition along the stonewall at Gettysburg:
the night breeze rustling its saber before they slept.

Philip Levine Expects Walt Whitman

The poet rises from his wobbly kitchen chair,
and looks around at the countertop with its vodka-
colored Formica, the chair with his coat flung over it.
There's a quiet like a cannon about to shout
with its balls and tangled wilderness of bloodshed.
His last book, *What Work Is*, remains on his right,
paged open to the poem about men waiting in line
for work, do you know what work is when you see
your brother there, his huffed eyebrows, collar
turned up for the cold air of the industrial city?
He wants to fight for his book with Whitman,
a wind sweeping his right hook to the famed Brooklyn ferry,
sit down for a good game of chess: white or black,
the orchard of hands will ask, its knuckled apple
about to be placed onto the chessboard.
The Detroiter with middle age seeping into his bones
dreams he's lying wounded in a Civil War battlefield.
But war's a dangerous road, and the one-time
factory worker listens to WJR like he always
manages every night to soothe the mysteries
he can't ever figure out. Brittle sounds emerge
from the darkness of his one-hundred-year old house
like a limping burglar, who suddenly dances
these icy glittering steps, come to rob a poet of his mind.
If it's Franny, his wife, he will take her into his arms,
and be a master to his personal oblivion,
but mostly now it's solitude beside an empty chair.

Billy the Kid in a Phone Booth

Billy the Kid splashed water over his head,
and shivered when he heard the shadow
of footsteps near him in the starlight.
A slowness invaded his bones, hearing
the sheriff whisper, thinking of the men
already dead: twenty-two notches.
Let the future shoot me through the heart,
Billy said, looking at the cool water barrel
and thinking of his mother's eyes, like a rattler
wanting to bite Billy with her love—
one of two boys she couldn't feed.
But the New York boy heard Pat Garrett's
animal voice again. "Billy, I'm going to bite
you first, and you'll lay there wondering
if anyone ever loved a boy like you."
He had this feeling of some other world
where suddenly he was dialing a number
in a glass coffin looking out at his assassin.
His heart jangling like his black spurs
with their silvery nickel trimmed to his boots.
The voice on the other end of the phone
whispered its dark blizzard, and the sand
of the Mescalero Territory blew across
a shirtless Billy standing there on the porch,
where he had climbed out of Paulita's window
with tousled hair and that wild expression
as if he was about to taste death's true medicine.

Edgar Allan Poe Might Be Listening

These young faces misunderstand Allen Ginsberg,
who could be merely a lapful of oranges,
or Edgar Allan Poe's calico cat crawling out a window,
but surround him in his performance like an intruder
who needs to be watched carefully. He's loosened
his trousers for monsters his age; with his bearded
armor for reading late into the night, his eyes of an Underground
Room where a beautiful body sleeps behind a nailed
door that never opens. He's from the Bronx, where breath
measures prison sentences in a single sentence or two.
His audience is as blond as a blizzard outside growing
brighter as the wind guffaws and greets every stranger
who dares to venture out in this coldest winter on Earth.
We have brought our bearded monster over to the high school,
where Edgar Allan Poe's dancing on tiptoe past
the open pod for the poet from Hell. Poe's listening
with his eyes stretched over barbed wire and teeth
in need of a holy angel. The Ginsberg family did their
university reading, a beat dog laying out beside the son,
who was waiting for Louis, his father, to finish his Barcelona
rhapsody. His eyebrows must be connected somehow to death,
those minutes wasted in a hotel room, where he waits for his son
and their flight home to the tenements and flooded metaphors
found in coffee and accents from all around the world.
And when Allen stops singing, if it's really a song
or just a middle-aged man with no voice attempting
to step into Dylan's shoes, who perhaps doesn't
have a voice either, there's a silence that weighs
over two hundred pounds—and it keeps growing heavier,
as no one understands him or why he has fallen
from outer space like a meteor that's too hot
to touch. And then we're out in the truck again,
driving away like Kerouac in Centralville,
never looking back, his brother to catch;
and Allen's father pacing the floor of his hotel room,
his watch a death sentence strapped to his wrist,
wondering if his son will grieve for him when he's dead.

Postcard from Paris

for Jonathan Johnson

I was holding your postcard, which was small
as a driver's license with handwriting like matchstick ends,
attempting to read what you wrote about Shakespeare
and Company. I had not moved from my chair
and my eyes shone upon the ancient routes,
drinking coffee with your words. You told me

how the bookstore smelled of mold and coffee,
also relating that maybe dishes you heard clattering
into a sink were the bird-size bones of those writers
who once visited this famous bookstore not far
from the Latin Quarter or the River Seine.
Back in the cold of the Upper Peninsula,

I had been reading a Blaise Cendrars poem,
poet and painter with one arm from the trenches
who had penned "The Prose of the Trans-Siberian
and of Little Jeanne of France." He learned
how to paint one-handed, still a young man
who gazed out ice-crusted windows fascinated

by hunger cold plague cholera and the muddy
waters of the Amur carrying along millions of corpses.
The last train left Moscow, risking the Revolution
that liquefied villages. Little Jeanne, the whore,
slept beside Cendrars. Her body was strangely naked in his dreams
of alarm clocks and an assortment of Sheffield

corkscrews. And if you were a painter you'd splash everywhere.
I think we were all slightly crazy, Blaise wrote,
and that an overwhelming delirium brought blood
to the exhausted faces of my traveling companions.
But you, Jonathan, were just as crazy, sleeping
upstairs at Shakespeare and Company. Or that's

what I imagined when your postcard arrived.
You probably were sleeping in a hotel bed.
No words roared like a forest fire from poetry
you read. But, dear friend,
let's picture all the coffins from Malmo
filled with canned goods and sardines in oil,

and how the River Seine drifted along
with the currency of leaves,
and you could expect anyone to come walking up
to the famous bookshop, even a monk
from the seventeenth century,
looking at today's riches that floated beyond us.

His Canoe over the Watery Grave of Lake Superior

Beneath his frozen feet, a Bible wrapped up
in a faded brown cloth, a bag of flour spilling open,
not believing in heaven tonight, his paddle lifts above his shoulder.
He listens to the silver flash of sabers every time
lightning strikes the horizon, and some part of him
left behind at Cemetery Ridge climbs through his skin,
until he can't close his eyes without screaming.
A comb's tines running through uncut hair won't quiet
his sorrow now, nor will cutting scraggly sideburns

built into a small beard. No longer a boy, he leans forward,
knowing charging soldiers will line up in suspicious dreams.
Once ashore he'll meet the indifference of a bedroll,
but he'll breathe her name anyway, his blue-eyed girl
with wide hips, who, not even there, spoke quietly.
His throat vocalizes Freda, and falling snow flies
from his heart, or mumbled prayer for her
that no longer provides any sense to his ear.
His hopes are needle thin that he'll ever be loved,

and bobbing wildly he turns the canoe in a wide arc.
He imagines the cold as an angry woman.
Snow whirls round his shoulders in the shape of her.
Her belly, this bowl of enormous cold white flesh,
and the insane pain of her twists his intestines.
Lightning will open the graves where the dead sleep.
He had paddled so far away from Cemetery Ridge,
and the startled look of his girl when she said goodbye.
Her letters bundled up and tied in his rucksack make him
ache every time he uncrumples one and finds his heart.

III.

Philip Levine on His Last Poem

How many stars were shining outside?
He'd written about Detroit again, Chevy Gear
and Axle at dawn. His youth oily under his work shoes
he removed when he returned home
to his Jewish mother. Her eyes still the same
child's blue that wasn't blue but this color
of mercy and the Detroit River.
He'd remember a starlit evening
when he stripped to baptize himself
in the brine and auto parts with a Polish girl
from high school, their limbs flashing
white on that spring's dark chrome
celebration of everything sexual.
He wanted his hands to take him home,
and raised them above his head with hair combed
over his ears' radar, listening for Franny
to wake and tell him he wasn't dead.
When he heard a voice talking to him from
the refrigerator's hum, it was a soldier
from the Spanish Civil War who murdered Lorca
with a bullet to the back of his head.
Federico had dug his own grave first, wiped away
his sweat on a shadow of himself before he fell
into the black earth. Franny finally awake, the sheets
sticking to her skinny legs. If he stopped for a moment,
he'd feel the soft cement of the Ramblas
and hear heaven in these pigeons of Barcelona.
Maybe Miles Davis breathed a high note
on his trumpet to clear the industrial filth in Detroit.
If he could only hear a jazzman say our next tune
will be of your heart, and the heart will not quicken.

Like Any Strange Thing He Is Unsure Of

a French meal eaten after midnight to the piano
of Thelonius Monk, or insistent rain upon

the roof tapping out a code on his skin,
this girl with large hazel eyes he wants to keep

longer. He hears her voice in its murmured whisper,
that space before them like water as he rows

her hips to a private bed. This synchrony
comes from real life, like a want or ache

he can't put back together right; even
if he's dreaming still, he's unsure of the secret

in her roots, her short blonde hair ruffled,
what he can't tell to another as he removes

his fingertips and tastes champagne.
He has never seen her face before,

and as strangers they kiss deeply that tangerine
of their lips. Their bodies are sweet butter

melting, and in a dream they never hear
what desire's meant to say, if anything,

before dreamtime's over and a mirror
drinks the sugar bags under his wide-awake

eyes, teeth in their curious yellow grin,
sorrow caught in his face he couldn't ever erase.

Julian Lennon at the Morrison Hotel Gallery, New York City

Private Premiere of His Photographic Exhibition
"Timeless," September 16, 2010

His father's long hair grew slowly
like their estrangement, and was cut short
after the Beatle years. Julian, a shadow
in his father's life, a boy used to absence.

Up on the wall at the Morrison Hotel
are photos of Sean, heavily bearded thoughts
of John seen in those chin curls, his big smile
more like Lennon on the Ed Sullivan Show,
bursting with rock and roll.

In Julian's own middle-aged face he sees
his father hiding, all his fears
in a celebrity smile that has shades
of a sneer, the older brother celebrated
as a photographer, but he remembers

Julian, the boy, swimming in the ocean
with his wet-eyed father caught in May Pang's
lens, who ate hot dogs on the beach
and was shown chords by his dad
on the guitar, its belly full of sand.

"I have always felt I have observed life,"
he says to his champagne glass,
expecting nothing in return, his wrinkled
face older than his father when he died
from bullets that made his assassin famous.

Julian, his hair receding, worn long over his collar,
steps in his father's shadow on the gallery floor,
all his father's wives there to be hugged,
his hands buried deep into their pockets,
head down and suspecting the worst of fame.

Dead Man's Float

Jim Harrison mulls over the woman beside him
who keeps withdrawing her hand.
The TV's on but he observes the universe
like everybody else with dead eyes.
She tells me to entertain their literary guest
at the hotel, where I work as a night porter,
and she escapes from her barstool. He's dreaming
of a seventeen-course gourmet meal that he ate in Paris,
with his partner who could have been Hemingway.
He segues to a story of Zelda Fitzgerald with her hair
of soft curls in a chin-length style, and the films
F. Scott never managed to get down on paper
in his Hollywood office where Thalberg imprisoned him.
I'm sitting next to Brown Dog, Clare who decided
at a rest stop along Interstate 80 to leave her husband,
or the many incarnations of a poet in search of small gods.
No introductions are necessary, with my disheveled hair
and bulky sweatshirt: my hands are greasy from washing dishes.
No suckling pig for me or French wine imported at a hundred
dollars a bottle, his addiction lurking somewhere in his spleen,
but I follow his one eye as it flickers over Mulligan Creek,
the dragonflies skimming the velvet surface of stagnant water.
Harrison's offering me a vodka to kill time, as if it were
a beautiful blue-eyed woman, always bare-breasted.
He's talking about the Riviera and skinny dipping
with Zelda in a dream. He's over his head
in the water, but you can see he's not drowning,
spreading out his arms in a dead man's float. A city of stars
interrogating him as he splashes to shore. He says he's fond
of blood sausage, connecting eternity to his overfed belly
wondering if he could have dinner in the afterlife
with the Spanish poet, Antonio Machado, forsake forever
an empty plate of hunger. Number the stars like notches
on his belt. His health may be threatened by alcohol, appetite,
and American Spirits, but he can eat his way out of any life.

Beside the Breakwall near Five-Foot Splashing Waves

Sailboats up on blocks like little hotels
propose a place for ghosts who never
left behind their desire to be free of land.
Moored to the parking lot, they tremble
in the eternal snow of the stars,
their masts rattle with claws
that no longer grip metal: the hull
in its visible stillness forever seen now
for those walking by, who compare
these guestless interiors to their own
secret places where they don't want to be seen
as frozen feet filled with a heavy sorrow
of those who have never left their cabins.

Electric Mudman Moon

He was saying to himself, "Take note, look very close
at Jackie Duluoz and Lousy in this nightmarish neighborhood."
In the waving high dark of the deep Pacific rollers,
Jack pretended he was a detective in a pulled-down rain hat
and meandered out to the ridge of the dreamy meadow.
He had to look at everything for clues to his holy existence
including a woman preparing for an ocean swim.
Her name was Romana Swartz, a Romanian
stripper who was staying with them at the cabin.
Duluoz was his and bemoaned his fate as an alcoholic,
who heard the rollers carom off the rocks, slippery logs,
mosses, big dangerous trees leaning over the ocean,
and was afraid of the aerial roaring mystery in the dark.
His maman wrote of little Tyke's death in a letter
that lay crumpled in his shirt pocket. His Persian cat
whom he wrapped around his wrist like a furry thing
he loved to pet. He loved all animals, his brother Gerard
would say, and he would need them in his absence.
But Tyke was gone. He had spent a week on his own
drying out at Monsanto's cabin, but foolishly hitchhiked
back to San Francisco. He'd returned drunk with a carful of others.
Lorenzo, whose real name was Lawrence Ferlinghetti,
knew it was no good for Jack to sit alone with his knees up
listening to the giant waves in their tragedy. Like Orson Welles,
or somebody with his heart in his pants, he watched
as a hundred birds circled above his battered fedora
and couldn't forget poor Tyke wrapped around his wrist.
Duluoz in a walking prayer for everything holy
stumbled away through the meadow, surprising some hawks
that lifted up into the sky, as if his prayers were broken
and flying away without having said them first in his heart.

Baseball and Minié Balls

Cemetery Ridge, July 2, 1863

An Arkansas man on his bugle signaled
Union soldiers to play; they'd been cooking
chicory for their morning drink; now they cast
their tin cups down as battered gloves.
A ball pounded into old leather demonstrated
that this union of man and baseball could hold.

Shiny sabers stuck into ground and billed caps
like feisty bluebirds danced off, enough room
for the diamond dug out with shovels.
General Meade watched from a distance,
not thinking of an attack today, as his tired steed,
Old Baldy, strained through its nostrils.

The first batter, a boat builder from Maine,
his giant biceps flashing in the Gettysburg sun,
aligned his body beside the sack that was home plate.
"Come on, batter, look where his fastball
can't see you are hiding," cried General George
Armstrong Custer on deck in the blowing dust.

A red-haired hurler called the Butcher
volunteered to take the mound; how
he held the ball as if it were an egg
stolen this morning from a farmer's chicken
coop; he spilled that blue wine of his next breath
while he lifted his hands above his head.

Not in prayer, but this wind-up he was
stitching from burning muscles, and he waited
for the egg cracking its cacophony
into the catcher's mitt like a promise broken.
How the batter's empty swing would only
fester with his mouth pursed into a wound.

The Butcher got the ball back from the squatting
catcher, who swore to the boat builder
he'll never see the daylight of the next pitch,
as the Butcher turned his back on the batter,
and kept right inside him the faces of all
his brothers who lay dead in the nearby field.

The Last Tumultuous Avalanche of Light above Pines

He was wounded on a Civil War battlefield
somewhere below Little Round Top
of Gettysburg and he would die, his wife's
name like a gasp from his torn chest.
His letters would be collected from his pack,
next to an uneaten orange and her letters;
mostly unread because he had been saving them
for after the battle with General Meade's men.
They would end up at the Burton Historical Society,
and one rainy afternoon a Detroit poet
would sit down at a table and think of the Union soldier
that was him, Private Orlando Metcalfe Poe,
twenty years old and from Michigan,
serving with General George Custer. The crashless
fall of time when cannonballs echoed, and the next day
would become the future. Then the Jewish man
whose raincoat was still wet from taking the bus
began copying a letter. The soldier's voice
caught him rising before dawn, writing
as he stared out the window at Gratiot Avenue.
Let the stars become my ink, that mess
of a heart. He would be late for the factory,
if he delayed any longer at the historical society.
His galoshes stared at him below the table.
He didn't know if Orlando would die that day,
or the latter part of his letter to his wife would reveal
her roundness, as if that part of her was sexual,
like a dark nub rushing across crinkled pages.
The Jewish poet sat stunned, afraid if he read
more he would see his own death before long.
He thought of Stonewall Jackson, the Rebel
General who had died before Gettysburg.
Then Robert E. Lee watching an evening hawk
like a bullet scar upon the sky in its winged geometry.
His head whirling from the future, shadows
running away from him, darkness a final wind
that even the moon couldn't clear until morning.

A Thousand Cares Dispelled in Starlight

sweeping down to bend back
the loose boards of a collapsed porch,

as if no weight of foreclosure
was too heavy for the stars to fix.

The Mojave seems like a photograph
slowly developing if you walk

out among the stars, leaving the car
running for your headlights to guide

you past the barrel cactus,
without caressing its endpoints,

standing like a stranger you didn't expect.
But now something cold and unclear

riffles a strengthening current.
The road addresses the world's

troubles with this spectacular glow
that reaches the clumps of Yucca

towering over the scrubland flora
at night. A cosmic neon touches

behind a fence the silver
of a cow's otherworldly skull.

Hotel Room, Fourth Floor, Old Marquette Inn

The only way to stay out of trouble is to grow old, so I guess
I'll concentrate on that. Maybe I'll live so long I'll forget
her. Maybe I'll die trying.

—Orson Welles as Michael O'Hara walking away
in *The Lady from Shanghai*

I didn't say her name for a week because it made me
think of her living with a family in Paris.
I had fled from her brassiere factory
reading Kenneth Koch's poetry in a double bed.
Her brassieres were works of art, large murals,
and they grew larger over the years.
My bright star was in Paris and I was at the hotel,
on the fourth floor looking out at Lake Superior
from my small square window where we left
milk to keep cool. Mister Marshall fumbled for things
unseen behind our shared thin wall; he cranked
up his TV when my Smith Corona rattled on too loudly.
He hadn't thought of breasts in a decade.
I lived next door and wanted her back.
I would never see her again, imagining her in love
with some French boy who puffed away
on clove cigarettes, and those brassieres in poems
by Kenneth Koch reminded me of a listless factory
where they were first sewn. Cups of all sizes,
even though Koch's poem wasn't about breasts at all.
I wondered what bare breasts might be if not under
a lyric poem bouncing and rushing into poetry all its own.
I was working as a night clerk, answering calls
on the switchboard. I couldn't help but think of a brassiere
factory or why Kenneth Koch wrote about one.
One week some strippers checked in, and Frenchella Jones
described her act of dancing with whipped cream
and nothing else, leaving her plucky nipples last to be licked.
I never opened her forgotten suitcase. But imagined

the simple life of a girl from Iowa, perhaps, who
took up a career of pole dancing, where breasts
were a prison, if you gave them too much thought.
One night I connected Tripoli to a resident who missed
his call by not being in his room. But that fellow
in Tripoli wouldn't hang up, and after my shift I watched
The Lady from Shanghai. I thought of the Funhouse Mirror,
faces doubled up until bullets eliminated all but one,
Rita Hayworth's character collapsing
in her real husband's arms, Orson Welles,
whose voiceover on the Carnival Ground escaping her
would haunt me, even as I remembered it now,
as if all along I had been the man holding the gun.

Beat Poet, Beat Dog

When the great poet in a sports jacket
reads, he parts the air about to tighten
around his throat at the lonely podium.

Let me sprawl beside his son plopped
on the gym floor, a Beat poet beside me,
a beat dog, dreaming of chasing an animal

through the snowy yards of his neighborhood.
Some one hundred and fifty people away
from the stage, my floppy hound tail beats

to the older poet's beat of his own soundless war,
talking about how bombs burst over Barcelona,
and where my master is I don't know

but the girl on the other side of me ruffles my fur
the right way and I am not moving, not now,
her distinctive nose still arousing my interest,

her roundness of form like a Renoir.
And her dogged look staring at the old poet
behind the podium reminds me of love

my master bestows in my bowl of table scraps,
and I feel there is something missing here
like a bone not where it's supposed to be.

And it's my master who has left me
to hit on a girl across the gym floor.
His eye in orbit around the expanse of the room,

the old poet finally eyeballs his son there,
hair to his shoulders and oracular
in his scraggly, uncombed beard,

or maybe he did comb it that morning
in his hotel room they shared,
but his fatherly eye missed it.

It will be me on the front page with Allen;
and the caption reading: *Beat poet, Beat dog*:
and it will be me, that canine everybody loves.

The girl beside me has red hair
to her shapely shoulders, a luxurious body
hinted at beneath a winter sweater.

If she understood dog language, she'd know
my high intelligence as my head turns
and buries its snout between my legs:

an idiosyncratic hound who reads poetry,
stirred by a Ginsberg laying out what happened
to poets in another generation.

His son who will read next, so fully alarmed
at the attention his very Jewish father
is getting, shifts his improbable butt

and sighs dangerously; like always,
the son must follow his father leaning
on the podium, his billboard presence

bigger than he would like, but I am reminded
of the night with all its strange smells, the snow
outside discolored just right for me to sniff.

My Night with Marilyn

My mother-in-law read James Joyce
when the sleeping pills didn't work,
hoping that so many words
from *Ulysses* would put her to sleep.
A big fat book slightly frayed around the dust jacket
with its banner of red through the cover.
This Modern Library Giant was the same
as the one Marilyn Monroe was reading.
When I caressed those chapters
I thought of Jane propping up the giant copy
against her chin, but then I saw *Ulysses*
on Marilyn's nightstand. Her body
was not wrong for a sex star
who was fifty pounds overweight;
she must have admired the bold chocolate-
eating Molly with her Spanish blood.
Her wet lips that parted red,
her blonde hair sinfully uncombed,
always miscast in movies as the bimbo.
Old James Joyce was passed around
from one sleepless woman to another,
who couldn't resist. I fell in love with
Marilyn night after night seeing
her in bed with a book, her legs
shifting under the sheets. Alcohol
with the starry night outside, and her body,
these exploding points of the Milky Way.

Sweat Lodge

One of those mornings my fever
seemed unsure if I would sweat.
Believe me, I was okay with less wear and tear
on my sleep—I had not gone to it—sleep, that is,
which was a problem. I'd stayed up all night
watching *The Night Manager*, wondering
what Jonathan Pine in his spydom was capable
of, in this John le Carré spinoff of his fiction,
selling weapons to the highest bidders.
He played a character with multiple selves,
and had to choose which one to sleep with Sophie's ghost,
his Sophie who'd been brutally murdered
in the Cairo Hotel, and which preyed on my mind
and my fever too—seemingly burned out
that morning. To defy my health, I drank wine,
allowing gravity to curl me in a sleeping bag. I said goodbye
to my wife in the hospital, where they told her
she had influenza. I went home for an illicit evening
with Tom Hiddleston, in *The Night Manager*,
in the title role, and Hugh Laurie as his nemesis,
the evil Mr. Roper, watching on the floor
in my sleeping bag. Soon the fever entertained
me with her clinging form. Fever was busty,
her wide hips settling upon mine. I cranked up the heat,
not knowing what to expect. Maybe I'd build a sweat lodge,
let fever do what she wanted. I was a breathless
old fool in love with her kisses and frightened of dying.
Fever wanted me all to herself, her fingers inside me,
prying open my mouth. But there was no air.
My face a mess of perspiration, under my arms
swollen, tongue thick and heavy, in a mirror naked,
spread-eagled on the floor, my skin on fire, my thoughts
a muddy river impossible to swim.

Kafka in Love

He eats a mouthful of black bread,
enough to nourish
a singing mouse.

A woman offers soup.
He looks for the stones, twigs
that hurt his throat.

He swallows
after watching the hairs
at the back of her neck
stand up.

If she strokes his body,
four strings vibrate
and his voice squeaks,
"Hand me a pencil."

He scribbles with a nub
as his mistress demonstrates
movement of her shoulders,
unbuttoning her dress.

At Eighty-Two, a Shadow of Himself Fights the Younger Leonard Cohen

To write any poem was hard,
and the clock biting minutes told the rounds:
Look how I am bleeding when I remember Marianne.
Head hung low, three claps of thunder in a row,
as my words fought for the center of the ring.
I was losing my touch, wasting so much of my shadow
running around trying to catch an incomprehensible
bit of scribble I'd written on foot in Montreal.
I was young then and able to beat myself up pretty good,
but nothing like this older man who wears precisely
angled hats, dapper in suits, his fame certain now
like tattoos that won't erase, and who sings
with an uplifted hand, expecting applause to fill
his outreached grasp. I lost my voice to women
too many times, and looked for my Marianne.
I had once said goodbye to her years ago.
Her hair long as a rope from which I wanted to make
my noose, laughing at the idea when we were so young.
I was up against a heavyweight with raven eyes
and twice the reach, even if he was stooped and spoke
sweetly of everything that died, including Marianne.
A look of a killer if he wanted to be, for he had sung the song
of Isaac tested by the Lord. He knew how to be wise,
to jab where he thought the gut was; to cajole
in that dreamy, gravelly voice of darker things;
and caught me with a poetic hook, everything
I wanted to borrow from his endless rewriting.
To make Joan of Arc's death so beautiful the older
Leonard would never be able to touch her.
To perspire with her in love and light, to praise
her name as if it was the only one. Leonard Cohen
was punching me out, as if he objected to me
using a flake of his song. He never wanted
me to drink from that cup of darkness.

Teaching Poetry at the Prison on Thursday Nights

How they stare up at the lonely moon
frozen above them like a clock
through the classroom windows.
They are killed by time, men whose
murders bristle under their skin.
Let me be their teacher is my hymn,
walking through the gate
operated by a sharpshooter
who stands over in a tower
and waves back with his reluctant
waggle of fingers, making sure
the poet can see him catching flakes of snow
as if each one were key somehow
in entering this prison gate
with an uplifted hand.

I told them as a young poet
how I couldn't read my future
anywhere but through poems,
startled how powerful they looked
when I pulled them out of my pocket,
tasting their sadness on my lunch break,
usually a job that never lasted
longer than a week.

Let the smallest of poems
be a crack in some wall they can escape
through and ride a bus downtown
and see young girls in their minis.
These prisoners face the poet
who has never looked so alone,
pacing in front of the class,
as they wait for him to keep silent
for them, to dream of the men
who put them there as killers.

Ferlinghetti Walking to the Caffe Trieste

Likely in tennis shoes for that lighthearted
cadence moving past shop after shop,

his eyes on a birthday cake from a pâtisserie,
chocolates with hearts of syrup, Lawrence

kicks over mattresses on Columbus Avenue.
A phantasm of a bloody canine barks at a French

restaurant just opening, as if conjured
by Edgar Allan Poe, and this hundred-year-old poet

born in Paris and raised by his Aunt Emilie
strides faster only because he can.

He walks toward the Caffe Trieste,
parting pedestrians in his world of blindness,

his hands lost in pockets but pulls them out
for balance to veer from an overturned chair

in a curb guttering with garbage. On a bright
Saturday afternoon, because you feel lucky

to be alive, you obey the margins of the sidewalk,
hoping not to stray into traffic.

Picture him a tall Charlie Chaplin,
tipping his eyebrows to strangers.

His pork pie hat doffed to a blur
of womanhood that passes by him.

The great illusionist at his age of a hundred
defies death by strolling down

Columbus Avenue without wearing
underwear and his shoelaces untied.

IV.

Terminal

Picture me walking down Sunset Boulevard
observing my fat shadow splashed
across the sidewalk. I notice the homeless
have put on weight as I adjust my sweater vest
with a tug. Then tip my Irish cap
to strangers who pass without even a nod.
I glide toward the coffee shop around the corner
carrying poetry in my pocket, and hope
a few vertical lines in a notebook will bear
up later, under scrutiny. These words
like dust blow away from my moving lips,
talking as if I were an out-of-work actor
carrying his own Macbeth. There is no explanation
except I am a bad poet visiting Hollywood,
whose windmills are huge as they spin around
when I depart to the security of a café: semi-bustling.
Those cars like combatants I have to face
crossing the street down to Vermont Avenue.
I mug for the pedestrians approaching me
in morning traffic: a poet wearing
a hat in the heat. My eyebrows yawn
under my spectacles, with useless factories,
endless filling stations, and bars,
my Midwestern look of a martyr, walking
to get to the other side of the street
with a Latino doctor and his handsome brown eyes,
movie good looks, a nametag bouncing
against his white shirt, right here before
the Children's Hospital, who with a lifted
gaze perhaps diagnoses me, the poet, as terminal.

The Dream Radio's Dialed

Somewhere in Malibu Tom Petty lays
his guitar down. His hair the whiskey gray
of the Florida bayou. Last night he played the Hollywood
Bowl, tonight he rides a moon above
billboards, as if he senses this road will be the last one.

There may be sudden turns in his heart he wishes
he has never taken; and he glances over at Roy Orbison
in the passenger seat of his dream convertible:
donning black apparel and large sunglasses
to shield him from the world, Roy nods his head

to the last turn in the road down the canyon,
a little too fast for him; the radio's destroying his heart
with the past, one of his early hits, "Pretty Woman."
Soon they're driving Topanga, as if none of the LA
miles mean any more than a dream.

And the Jaguar, cushions soaked in the hot broth
of a California early evening, crescendos through
searing gears toward the ocean. George's walking
along Oceanside, his Beatle hair a mop again.
And he crawls in on top of Roy, his guitar clutched

to his chest, and they decide to head for the desert.
The needle of the gas gauge never moves from empty,
but the dream radio's dialed in right,
and the ocean breeze still smells sweet for a while behind them;
they're bound to find the sound they're looking for.

Levon Helm Sings for All the Virgil Caines

Your dream address can be anywhere
down any rail of regret.
A train whistle far away but close
as a heartbeat buried in song.
In defeat, Virgil Caine can't dig back up
his Confederate brother, killed by
a Yankee bullet, reminding you of your lost
brothers, in mud and blood of Vietnam.

Now that war rests heavy on your shoulders,
your dream address leaves you face to face
with all the Virgil Caines. The demeanor
of those who have given blood and mind,
have eyes vacant as empty houses.
Their teeth like fences needing mending.

You want to tell them something
about taking the best from a generation
and your refusing to relent,
the letter that saved you from the draft.
You breathe through your eyelids,
as if a mystic suddenly, at the Café Paradiso,
a name you made up, for the heaven of it,
and sitting there alone with a bitter coffee
you listen to that dream train
split its whistle cry apart, and collect
the shards into a glittering rail of song.

Dead River

She parks near the bridge
where we walk down to the Dead River,
its banks crowded with sticks blown
off the lower branches, us clinging to the loose
sleeves of each other's bulky coats.
We watch the milky froth swirl
in currents, while her long walnut-colored
hair flaps across her face.

She slides off a glove to dip fingers
into freezing water. Like lost children
they wander over my body, finding
bare skin where my collar opens at the neck.
Both of us are thinking how our love
appears to be that cold water spilling
nowhere but over ancient moss of rocks.

Our loneliness left threshing like geese
in their flight or a marsh hawk as a predator
scavenging over the wild grass.
But down by Dead River on slippery
stones, night comes unknotted
and headlights peer across the old stone bridge.

We resemble the homeless who take shelter
in the falling snow. The geese, our strange
companions, depart above empty branches,
and we look down at the lacy foam of the river
bunched up against the neck of the shore.

The water with its frozen grin whirls on
in indifference. We stand back, unable to hear
the snowplows tell us the road is now clear,
that to touch is to forget everything we know.

Beneath the Vulture's Slow, Circling Motion

Marilyn Monroe hopes her breasts will work
their way into the next scene as a divorcee;

her Lee Rider jeans caught from behind
with the second camera, as if they knew her body

on the salt flats of Nevada could bounce
like a trampoline and make her a star again;

a woman who at thirty-six has nothing
to lose—the one thing she never had was love.

Orphan child abused by her many fathers,
she stares upward at the circling vulture.

A one-piece bathing suit clings to her; she'd worn it
mincing out of the frigid Pyramid Lake,

her breasts bouncing as she ran.
Her miscarriage scars weren't visible.

Up above comes the one propeller prop
flown by a veteran chasing the remaining

mustangs where the canyon narrows;
she knows they'll be killed for pet food.

Montgomery Clift, low to the ground
like a wrestler, uncoils his lariat for the horses.

Marilyn throws her fists at the cowboys, calling
them murderers, but they don't understand.

Her sad mouth, the one that studied lines
with Paula Strasberg in New York,

droops at the corners, like a wilted
chrysanthemum, some nocturnal animal.

He Wants the Boy in Himself to Emerge
as He No Longer Soars above His Shortcoming

Richard Manuel keeps hoping
for the preacher to save him, preach gospel
that might stop his suicide, for heaven
is in the chord structures built
as if he were Ray Charles, but the bottle
atop the dresser in defiance of the boy inside him
says no to his slouching hawk figure at the piano.
His father was a mechanic at a Chrysler
dealership, in Stratford, Ontario,
where Shakespeare must have brushed
against his shoulders one night and the Bard
strengthened his baritone with that holy madman's
voice singing through a tempest.

The piano with its suspicions of Richard
rocks louder than it should, words
coming out all wrong despite him
fighting to remain himself in his gospel
of sorrow: the preacher in his black coat
absent from the swirling notes on stage, a broken
melody from Richard's piano on one
of their Big Pink songs with Bob Dylan.

The noose is all that's left for him
later that night, he had been thinking it for days,
his belt looped around his neck in the shower stall.
His body not to be washed clean ever again,
but carried out on the shoulders of the others,
Levon Helm weeping in the moonlight
of the parking lot, he's not dead they say,
that bearded brother who died from the rope,
we're carrying the child he once was in his father's eyes.

625 Palisades Beach Road

Nobody's going to age well in the California sun
and he wants to pick crazy chords
lost years ago in "A Hard Day's Night,"

that mammoth chart-busting opening
riff that led to the stampede of fans;
after John empties his Gibson of sand,

he plays to the effortless circles
of a mad geometry in the sea gulls
who know somehow the rock star won't last.

His girlfriend, May Pang, fingers her shutter
to catch John's long hair blowing across
madly freckled shoulders.

He can't see farther than the white dress
of the waves, Yoko falling down in shock,
and a fan who sank too far into fandom

to ever come back. May Pang kneels barely
in any clothes behind him—both are thin,
for sorrow's that diet which eats all fat.

And she loves Lennon, but knows
in his darkness he'll return to that other
who waits for him in New York.

And that's where he'll die,
and so if there's a heaven, it must be here,
as he begins singing a song for Julian,

who's visiting from London, the surf
out there imitating a drum solo,
from which he emerges wide-eyed

and wanting his father to love him,
John strumming strongly that love
as his boy empties his ears of ocean.

May shuttering father and son
with her Polaroid, as if fame doesn't
matter like this moment that will hang from a wall

at an exhibit in San Francisco at the Hotel
Zetta—Julian wet and wrapped in a towel,
Lennon the father in his troubadour cap

trying not to look like a Beatle or maybe trying
too hard to be famous anyway—
May Pang with her eyes big behind granny glasses

slipping down her nose, her shoulders
a fine texture of brown from windswept beach,
that loneliness the size of fame itself,

as paparazzi in helicopters fly over,
and he sips that first coffee to stop the chorus
of traffic driving across his back.

Henry Zender at the Fifth Avenue Hotel

There is music on a piano louder
than it should be this morning,
and he misses his slender, slightly emaciated
wife who clenches her broom as if cleaning
attics for God, who would know what
to say gazing upward at this mural.
That's what the mustached man
behind the desk calls this religious
vision of so many men at work,
including even the ghostly face of Lenin.
Henry from Detroit stands frozen
in his heavy coat and in his hand
holds his Borsalino, expecting Ty Cobb
to show up after a baseball game
in the Bronx. His cheekbones riding
high on his Georgian face, his voice
dropped low in its passage of curses
when a Yankee fan grabs him
by his buttonholes. He asks the desk clerk
where he should sign for his room,
and he addresses the ledger page
with a solitary finger touching
where his name should go.
Henry signs for an eternity,
stops only when he wants to be
anywhere but here recalling a heron
like a messenger from God
above the Detroit River.
He longs for his wife's wet kiss
on his cheekbone, her breath
this timelessness like an evening
hawk about to swoop down. His black hair
remains uncombed since removing
his wide-brimmed hat, held in his hand
as if his traveling companion.

But in the hotel mirror where he sees
himself full length, he wonders if he looks
more like an emigrant who speaks only
a language of immense sorrows.
Henry can smell the cigar smoke
of President Ulysses S. Grant
who began his campaign at the hotel.
The dead of the Civil War, not too far
behind him, and with a quill of some sort,
Grant signed for his room, and Henry
does the same, doffing his Borsalino,
a single battered suitcase like a fallen star
dripping in darkness brought up
to his arms, as he looks to ride
up the elevator to the starry night.

Entering the Classroom Benjamín Otálora

notices the blackboard hasn't been erased.
Mr. Palomar looks up from his desk
that he punishes with so many spilled coffees every day.

Benjamín, the janitor, with a low brow
and ingenuous light eyes watches the poetry teacher
sweep the pile of books into his arms,

volumes with torn covers, cigarette stained,
a Detroiter named Philip Levine,
who worked in an auto factory. Then sip

from a coffee cup that's still not empty
and stare distractedly at the future
as if he has forgotten something.

Benjamín about to reach for the board
turns to see the teacher's face of wrinkled folds,
like an old book himself–his white shirt

always dirty from leaning into metaphor.
He wonders what poem he chalked
today for him to sponge away.

Their eyes lock for a moment when Palomar
tells him he's sorry for the balled-up pages
of frustrated writers.

"See you tomorrow," he says, lowering
his shoulders, in his push toward the door.
When he's gone the janitor's heart stops

when he reads high up on the board
the first line of a poem by Apollinaire:
"In the end you are weary of this ancient world."

The Widower from Detroit

He saw her through the frost blossoms
of the window, her blue dress buttoned up
around her throat. The hunter who had driven
up from Detroit under the stars tonight
entered the café. He sat down in a chair,
dangling his extra wool heavy scarf
off its metal rung, as if it knew all along
his intentions: a double-barreled shotgun racked
in his Chevy. He ordered food from the waitress
bundled in an olive green shawl, her face
keenly intelligent, as she scribbled down
his order, then bowed deliberately to him,
an outsider with a grisly beard–a hunter
who would go to the woods and hunt for himself.
He spilled his cold hands over his lap to find
Detroit streets with names of Frenchmen
like Cadillac and Lafayette where his working
fingers grew scarred and small, the skin of a widower.
He searched for meaning in his wife's death,
the cancer that ate through her bones,
but only found this sunken version of himself,
elbows leaning on the table. When he looked up
from his ham and eggs, he recognized his love's
Russian face in the waitress who had been
watching him, her long nose and high cheekbones,
and the mouth an unsettled place
which could never stop talking. Except she
grew silent now. His Oksana away from home,
who saw him look at his empty plate of hunger,
scrape back his metal chair to take his leave.
She used that blade of a tongue to tell him be seated:
she didn't care about any wife dying in Detroit,
her nose all wrinkled and pointing elsewhere,
a coffee pot outstretched to offer him something warm.

This Wheel on Fire

This wheel on fire allows me to remember
the girl who slipped with me into the river
full of frogs and cicadas flying about her neck.
Her sunburned eyelids lowered as she gifted me
with her bare ass diving into the muddy mirror.
Believe me, old prophets of love and pestilence,
I always looked for redemption in her shoulders
of champagne and sunsets brightening her smile.
Richard Manuel grinning like a bear after writing
a song with Bob Dylan, and my hands reaching
for her body as if the heart were igniting this desire
wherever my fingers crossed. Let me find a laughing stream
to immerse our love and watch a thousand birds
circle the earth. A dog barks somewhere in the distance.
There's so much lost in an accordion rippling.
I feel thunder under my skin, walking down Parnassus Road,
wanting her arms wrapped around my shoulders.
All that remains for me is to walk until she appears
naked as the Old Testament, and her body to light
another fire on guitar, with Robbie dampening
the strings with the heel of his palm. There can be no true
path to love, but I keep hiking down Parnassus Road,
finding that I never loved her enough.

After Running Out of Gas on a Road in the Mojave Desert

Johnny Cash abandons his coupe, looks down
at the cholla cactus, as if it were his life
about to tumble away, and misses
his wife, June Carter,

who traveled ahead with the band
to Las Vegas, their luck running thin
even in the best of situations,
because of Johnny's pills and drunkenness;

and now he wants only to clean
those sins from his chest
by singing a good gospel song,
as he strides down the road.

Johnny Cash doesn't know
if wearing black will make him hotter
than a pepper sprout, but he's close
to finding out with his guitar over his back.

The sun above him like a record
that won't stop spinning the same song,
and he damn near faints, a chord played all wrong,
but so bright and yellow in the light,

as his pomaded hair topples across
his perspiring brow in an angry black curl.
Johnny, a jailbird whose wrong chords
kept him from the Lord,

will tell the first DJ
he meets at a radio station
about his desert walk, its inarticulate
spaces as confining as four walls.

At the Séance of Mrs. Kopitzky

Zorach wades through the labyrinth
of her apartment, watching his dream girl,
Nella, duck into a room.
Inside, he hopes it contains a toilet
but is unsure where he has entered,
his bladder not knowing any better.
He only received a single letter from her
after he emigrated to America. Her words like crows
sidestepping bodies, one of them hers
as it would end up. At the séance, he expects
little more than a warm room for an hour
or two of the foolish woman summoning
knocks on the table from dead people.
A telephone call interrupts the spirits
of the Heavenly Hierarchy. In the bathroom
Zorach meets Nella, or is it only a dream
he receives like old mail from an address
he no longer uses, the envelopes wrinkled
like him and full of words from the dead.
It is not Nella anyway but some older girl,
a stand-in for the séance. The dead are so
impatient these days. He raises his hands
to speak but she slips away. Back at the séance,
Mrs. Kopitzky, his personal medium,
her hair this nest of pins, color of changing
seasons, tells him the dead no longer
love him. But what is love except
endless coffee at the cafeteria,
the same old letters he reads from his wife.
His bladder interrupts any love, though,
needing to be relieved of the coffee.
The other girl waiting for him to make
up his mind in the next room, so she can
be summoned by the old woman's
fierce raps on the table.

On His Sixty-First Birthday the Music Repairman Danced a Tango while Dreaming of Cleopatra

Francisco Tadeo Isidoro hoisted his Willie Nelson
autographed guitar above his head, bumping into the chair,
like someone on a journey that would never end.
When the door was flung wide open to the weeping heat,
Mendez, that fat detective, swept away the shadows,
pointing his Webley-Fosbery at Francisco.
"I am here because your wife murdered Sergeant
Eusebio Laprida, and that guitar is mine."
His wife was traveling by bus across the border
to El Paso, staying with American friends.
The hapless sergeant lay buried in the hot dirt
of a Mexico City cemetery: his assault on Remedios
unforgivable to Patricia. "A bullet should stop your tango,"
Mendez spoke, rolling in with tumbleweed and heat.
Francisco savored timelessness in a sip of whiskey:
wild bees attracted to the charred white oak barrels
added an open air of honey to the elixir.
Mendez altered the aim of his Webley-Fosbery,
and foolishly moved toward the bottle on the chair.
He found a glass for his own drink, and hoped he'd dream
of a naked Cleopatra too, with her belly a circle of sun.
The Iraqi orchestra spinning on vinyl danced
like time itself. Whatever ancient Egypt was to Francisco
slapped across the wet floor with his bare feet,
his poster of Liz Taylor as the queen displayed for all to see.
His birthday would slip away again, like they all did,
older and never drunker than this on his homemade whiskey,
listening to the mad bandoneons who breathed out their bellows
from somewhere they would never return from.

One Day in May When I Opened Your Poetry

I have your book lying on top of Jim Harrison's
and I intend on paging through
In Search of Small Gods later,
not that it depends on raw garlic,
used tires, taverns, saloons, abandoned
farmhouses, lilac groves, wet sand
walked in bare feet, or a rebel moon
that leads its nightly charge outside
our window in a star-studded sky.

I'm hoping to be astonished at the right time
to determine the truth of poetry.
Dreams are fathered like my pillow
where I rest, not exactly dressed for anything
but your book's being played on top of my
belly's drum. I have lost twenty pounds
of wilderness through intermittent fasting.
Bees like bugles blowing their assault
around my tender ears, listening.

There are thousands of birds,
maybe only a hundred who have glanced
over at our balcony, waiting to see
my wife in her underwear or her naked husband
emerge from his bed, knowing my wife's
adjusting her brassiere for the bees
buzzing around her attracted to nectar.

I'm thinking of birds who have returned
back north, as if ghosts chattering
about their journey home. Then gravel roads
and girls, rainstorms, used oil smells;
love's trapped light at a gas station
where I worked when I was twenty-four,
pricking open oil cans to pour
upside down into an engine,
listening to the hood slam
somewhere deep inside my throat.

In Praise of My Wife on Turning Sixty-Five

Leonard's holding his favorite guitar at his favorite café
where he tells me her letters were read on a ledge
overlooking Mont-Royal, and he said
he was never brave to her, a face that any gypsy boy
could love and he could laugh and cry, requesting
the angels to pray for them. They met when
they were almost young and her round-assed
body of the best of painters walked around
his burning bush, not ready to step into his flames.
A Jewish boy now a grown man whose dark gray
pinstriped jacket serenades a knotted chord.
His cuffs are pressed by madmen with their eyebrows
plucked by the beautiful eyelashes of girls
running past him naked. Bagels about to be buttered
like a nightly sacrifice to cholesterol, and the drowning man
whose heart can never rescue him in each sanctified bite.
Leonard knows me well. I am every song he has wrung
from the neck of his black Greek E-guitar
as his hair catches fire and his black eyes silently burn.
Garbage and flowers, heroes in the seaweed,
listen now as he sings to a moon as cold as a new razor.
But some chords are just huge nudes painted
by D. H. Lawrence of lusty men and women.
They become more than chords with a famous blue raincoat,
fabric torn like chords in a minor key, not quite
there yet when he strangles the guitar's neck,
when he feels the shame that Isaac felt leading
his son to be sacrificed for the Lord.
Everybody needs that lonely secrecy
despite the gypsy man with his hair slicked back
in ecstasy at the café. His Jewish trance of yet one more song
busy at being born, and he lays down his guitar
that will be showcased in a Tel-Aviv museum.
We also have challah and Russian black bread,
a busty dancer of the dishes exclaims, her nipples

like guitar picks when there was only supposed to be
blind fingers finding the next song not yet composed.
Virgins and killers eating together, not knowing
how to give away what they longed to keep.

Sergeant Reese on Leave in Athens

He understood the weaponry of their fists
when his breakfast appeared before him.
His plate of kasha and steaming milk coffee,
olives lying there as if plucked from a monster's
head, not that Yanna was anything
but an Aphrodite barely clothed in a tight dress.
Her hair of black ringlets ablaze in the heat,
a short woman with her hips the center
of gravity. His sunglasses slipped from his nose
to envision a black boxer named Sugar Baby.
Their sweating torsos clinging to each other
when the awfulness of their future left them
breathless and with bloody nostrils, their teeth
damaged but still there. He should be talking
more about himself and Yanna together
on the floor in her Grecian temple of love,
more than Reese fighting Sugar Baby
in the Detroit warehouse ring.
Detroit was far away, and how the sandflies
sang of his blackness. He couldn't wipe
away that vision of Sugar Baby,
a black body glistening like Achilles,
and breathed in his jabs tossed one
after another, about to knock him down.
But Sergeant Reese wiping away the heat
on this morning in Athens grieved for his fellow
pugilist who had taken a bullet
for him plunging into the darkness
of a doorway in Fallujah. Lord, help us,
the coffee bitter but honeyed, and its taste
implored him to consider heaven
as he slowly celebrated his espresso.
And then he gazed up at a pale blueness
like a maligned canvas with its clouds.
If only he could stop dreaming

about Sugar Baby, for the Athens morning
appeared beautiful as Yanna's naked body,
but under her arms like the smog settling,
his usual waitress beaded with sweat.

All the Cars Honking Behind Us
at the Gas Station

I wasn't always that kind of girl who'd drive away
with her sunburned shoulders and sit there
in the bucket seat waiting for her boyfriend.
The pump boy's scrubbing our windshield of sins,
scraping off battered bugs from hell.
He's doing all the looking, with all the cars
honking behind us in a line that never ends.

We were already here but don't know when,
and my boyfriend asks for the dipstick
to be checked when it's so impossibly dark.
Look at it wobble in the air, like a dream
of something generous and wild and erect.
The boy in his wire-rims barely twenty
glances at me with my bare legs shaved
and sitting braless in the bucket seat.

We've got nowhere to go we haven't already been
and what's wrong with love, if this is love
with my boyfriend touching the pointed way
my nipples want to talk without ever saying a word
to his fingers, and he's telling that boy
whom we saw an hour ago to fill it up.
But he means only whatever change he rolls
in his hand like dice ready for another seven.

The black field of thistles where we laid down
now covers my short skirt and my breath
must smell of Southern Comfort, shared cigarettes
when his British sports car on its last legs
shone its headlights at our tangled limbs.
Maybe that boy's taking too long on the oil check,
his greasy rag hanging from his back pocket.

I don't look so bad in this strange faded neon light,
and if I am a little sore from sitting here, my heels
planted on the dashboard, it can't show.

Only this luminosity of beer, my skinny waist
like a plateau where my boyfriend likes to lay his head,
as if thinking of this strange dark universe
that was the marbled white flesh of a woman.

A Civil War Reenactor Walks into The Mason Jar

His unforgiven world at Cemetery Ridge
spills from his coffee cup like the blood
of so many men; his fingers fuss with his gray collar
of three stars, while Belle demands he take his smoke
into the parking lot where he has parked.
His weary bones remain at a table, though,
in defiance of everything he thinks.

Who could play him better than himself,
he decides, his beard a mass grave
for his mistaken attack on Union forces:
his loosely tied sash binds his potbelly so real,
some coffee drinkers must look twice
at the man with his generous wrinkles,
an old Confederate general, the one
who shows up in full costume
at the café on the highway.

He lives in his uniform with the double row
of buttons and billowing gray coat down near his knees,
one of the dead now too; he wears an empty
holster where a prop revolver once clung
to the fake leather—his hands flutter
across his three-starred collar again,
trying to decide to forgo his beverage
or walk deeply lost in his meditation
of thousands cut down in Pickett's Charge.

Crushing his cigarette out onto the Formica,
his hand like an evening hawk swoops
down his Confederate cap where out pours
that gray of middle age and his Rebels;
deep inside Robert E. Lee's eyes he sees
the remaining farmhouse full of holes
and the dead who would never march again.

He mumbles this prayer like an unstopped wound
in his throat, directs it to wherever
his feet carry him, and bends his head
to his dirty gray gloves, as if he has used them
in the garden more than on the stage.

The last Confederate scrapes his body
up from the cheap chair, and grins at Belle,
a young woman with rocket red hair
who mentions for him to think of her in another
reenactment; his voice empties coldly, not caring her eyes
are blue as the sky outside, nor that he can't
find the line he is supposed to say under his next breath.

The Last Photograph of Billy the Kid

Billy the Kid clutched a croquet mallet,
wearing a striped shirt and a busted hat.
Young Billy with his buck teeth and unruly hair,
whose father was dead in Kansas,
beat an egg ball across the cholla cactus,
its spherical oddity perhaps death
that rolled on forever across the ranch.
Billy brushed the cobwebs of his tears from his cheek,
thinking love felt like something lost.
But croquet was far from his mind
as he strode out onto the porch after bedding
Paulita. He heard footsteps speaking
from the shadows, and felt an itch
in his left hand without his six-shooter.
He saw himself in the mirror of the water,
as he drank from the rain barrel. Young Billy
who sucked fear from the moonlight
and wanted to crawl back into bed
with her body of some significance.
"I am watching you, Billy," he heard Pat
Garrett moan from the gravestones
that floated behind Billy's eyes.
He smelled death, a bitter iron taste
like a horseshoe flung into his face;
and a double-barreled shotgun poked
out from a shadow that the moon couldn't hide.
Billy somersaulted forward, the porch floor
covered in blood, and spattering the tail
of a black cat already up on the roof.

NOTES

6201 W. Third Street, Los Angeles, is the address of the Gilmore Drive-In Theater, where I imagine Richard Manuel and his wife Paula went to watch James Dean in *Giant*. The car crash Dean died in can't be ignored by the couple after Richard's multiple car crashes in Woodstock and now Los Angeles. James Dean takes on this mythical role of tragedy. Richard Manuel knows his wife wants to divorce him. This tragedy flashes its details like sudden fiction. "At the Gilmore Drive-In Where James Dean Up on the Screen Lifted His Arms Slowly" clocks the narrative in surreal times. The saddest part is that James Dean's death made him a legend right at the time *Rebel Without a Cause* and *Giant* were premiering.

* * *

"Letters Jim Harrison May Never Read" imagines the Michigan writer unlatching his mailbox in a wintry Grand Marais. He is a recurring character for me who enters my brain attic and rumbles around, his one eye always not knowing what to make of me. I first met Jim Harrison at the hotel where I worked as a night porter. I was a father with three sons and barely enough money to keep us afloat. I was told by my manager to entertain Harrison in the bar. He had been holding her hand captive for too long. Harrison, like that bunch of knotted rope Yesenin looped together, enters my subconscious world of apocryphal places. He thinks of a 37-course meal in Paris he helped prepare with other poets. The letters are spilling out of his mailbox:

one in particular from a woman down south who sends him photos of herself.

* * *

Walt Whitman is another dream figure for me. Through him I can see myself clearly as the older man I have become. But his voice looking upon the living crowd, the spontaneous nature of love, comes from a younger man. "Walt Whitman and His Lake Superior Baptism" sets a sense of place to my poetry, the sandy beach where seagulls cry out at any moving forms. It is a place where one strips his clothes to embrace the cold water–to share this baptism with another. Or if alone, to reflect upon one's life as it is immersed into the great lake. I have been there many times. All my life. When I walk on the beach, I look for Whitman about to wade into the waves and heal himself.

* * *

I believe in dream poems. In "Chagall Taught Me How to Drive" I seem to have been escaping from a Chagall painting while driving down County Road 550 with my pregnant girlfriend. There, with me, was Bella floating on her wedding day as painted by Moises Chagall. I was not the father to the child but a temporary lover. It was as if her sensuous belly and fingers pulling me closer around her curves taught me the road was to be driven in a different way. I had not driven in three years, but was glad to learn again. This poem is an exaggeration but with Lake Superior seen through the trees and animals like foxes or deer crossing the road it can be easily imagined.

* * *

Apollinaire is my muse. Modern poetry begins with his "Zone" and ends with his death from influenza after the Armistice. My mother was born that year. Her father died of influenza too. Apollinaire is an anchor for me that keeps my life from floating away. He is my mentor, my god who becomes an aerial torpedo. How many stars in their many tentacles on a northern night remind me of him and his tenderness. "Apollinaire at Walmart" takes him into the twenty-first century like a phantom rocket, a flare over no man's land, as he pushes his empty cart. Even his Calligrammes in their handwritten notations express the heart in their simultaneous nature of the subconscious.

* * *

In Paris Reese lives as an aging man who still loves young women. When he hears gunshots outside he arms himself for the battle, leaving a record playing on his turntable. "Miles Davis Playing on His Turntable" dreams of rebelling against old age, and Reese wants to shoot some sonofabitch with all his heart, and find that he's twenty again. His grandson writes of boxing, hoping his grandfather will be proud of his exploits in the ring. Reese wants to send a letter to his warrior grandson who served in Fallujah, and tell him everything about the dead that lay on the street and inside the concert hall. But he barely makes it down the avenue before he falls onto his face, for old age will kill him as good as any bullet.

* * *

The stripper at the Montreal club would never be forgotten by me. On the train from Sudbury, we had conversed with Carlos, a Brooklyn man who was meeting his wife in Montreal; it was he who suggested we go with him in a cab to a shoe store where they had rooms above to rent. Monsieur Gezo remembered Carlos, and when he looked at my girlfriend and me, as well as her one-year-old daughter, he told us there was a room. Carlos would get his own room: his wife was flying in from Nova Scotia and was a stripper who demanded her own dressing room at clubs. It was at one of those strip clubs where I saw a young woman strip to Joe Cocker's song, "You Are So Beautiful." And she was in "Montreal 1976." I would return to our room above the shoe store and recognize that same beauty in my girlfriend.

* * *

There was a coldness in love for many of D. H. Lawrence's poems. Hunger kept his pen busy on those long, unadorned pages. Love was something abstract as the waves breaking or the heat simmering on their roof. Their villa in Taormina was a refuge for a time. Frieda's fleshy body kept him at the kitchen table, writing and hoping to survive by his words. She propped her bosom on the kitchen table, reading letters from home. He couldn't help but admire her sunkissed flesh as her lips sucked the German from the letters. Then donning her sun hat, she pushed herself away from the table to walk out into the sun and aim her expansive bosom at its corona. Inside, he gazed through the villa window, the door open for winds that burst in from the balanced rocks, his wife sunbathing in a chair she dragged outside.

* * *

Robert Penn Warren was an early influence on me as a poet. His Civil War poems marched out of nowhere and into my life. His photograph on the back of his collection, *Now and Then Poems 1976-1978*, revealed a craggy, lived-in, and wrinkled kind of face that insisted you take his poetry seriously. Perhaps it was also because my young wife bought me this book when we were living in southwest Michigan. Two titles in my book were borrowed from him: "Bearded Oaks Made Dim Architecture" and "The Last Tumultuous Avalanche of Light above Pines."

* * *

"Downwind from Gettysburg" was a Ray Bradbury short story of a mechanical Abraham Lincoln who was assassinated onstage. One of John Wilkes Booth's ancestors felt it necessary to shoot the gears out of his head. That story got me thinking about a phone booth appearing in Fort Sumner, where Billy the Kid holed up with Paulita Maxwell. This futuristic phone booth was an essential image for my poem," Billy the Kid in a

Phone Booth." Naturally, it doesn't exist, but Billy falls out of his girlfriend's hacienda window for a drink of water. Paulita's brother has already betrayed Billy. He hears the phone ringing in the booth and answers it. The caller is Death, and Billy can't escape Pat Garrett's double-barreled shotgun.

* * *

Allen Ginsberg read poetry to the high school students, and my twenty-three-year-old self sat among them, wondering what to make of my Life. If I would ever become a monster like this mumbling William Blake. But all I wanted was love and my lover had jilted me for another. I let Kerouac drive through my head on his way to Centralville and all those other places in his imagination where Doctor Sax lurked in doorways with a mysterious count named Condu. "Edgar Allan Poe Might Be Listening" was what I thought as Allen spoke unreliable truths through his poetry on insanity. Somewhere I knew I would meet my girlfriend again and she'd offer me her body's roundness and all the other delights of her feminine grace. But we had to finish up at the high school and return to the hotel for Allen's father: there was a flight to catch back to the Bronx.

* * *

There is Hollywood to this vulture circling above Marilyn Monroe shouting murderers to the cowboys. She's isolated in the white space of a desert. She convulses violently to some inner music–and it was probably the sound of her voice under a boom mic. It is John Huston's artful cowboy film about a disintegrating western society. Arthur Miller wrote the script, and Marilyn was his wife throughout the shooting of the film. But just barely. She left him at the end, and Arthur connected with Inge Morath, one of the still photographers for the film. Marilyn would die, and he'd marry her. They had a daughter who would make a documentary of her parents. "Beneath the

Vulture's Slow, Circling Motion "portrays my obsession with Marilyn, her body in a swimsuit or a black skinny dress in her animal dance. Huston let the camera run, unsure what she would do. What she did was find an expression of her soul.

* * *

"Henry Zender at the Fifth Avenue Hotel" brings my great-grandfather to Manhattan. He was the father to my grandmother and great aunts. The Zender family lived on Zender Place, in a neighborhood of Hungarians, Austrians, and Swiss. His Zender Tavern was on Gratiot Avenue, across from The Historic Trinity Lutheran Church, built in 1850. Why he visited Manhattan is purely fictional, but a Detroiter wearing his Borsalino hat in the lobby surely feels uncomfortable without his wife Anna. It appears this could be one of many poems of Henry's experiences in New York. He died young, accidentally struck by a streetcar at Belle Isle. What Henry was thinking right before his death cannot be known. I like to think he was dreaming of his wife's skinny body in bed or his children's faces.

* * *

Ken Meisel told me of his visit to Big Pink, and I was walking down Parnassus Road with him to that strangely colored house. An unearthly pink, if you could call it pink at all, but think of Levon on drums, Bob Dylan upstairs in the kitchen typing up another song with all his misspellings. These compositions rose up from the basement in what would be called *The Basement Tapes*. One of them would become "This Wheel's on Fire," and that song burned through me remembering a loved one. I felt all the love I had for her preach to me somehow in a Biblical sense. There was a thunder under my skin with "This Wheel on Fire."

* * *

"Sergeant Reese on Leave in Athens" was suggested by a friend. It made sense he would be there. At the outdoor café Reese, a battered and soulful soldier, took in the morning vibe with Yanna, a young woman with the blackest hair ablaze in the sunlight. I made Reese remember Sugar Baby, his boxing opponent back in Detroit who had died in an ambush in Fallujah. Sugar Baby now became mythic as Odysseus perhaps as Reese ate Greek olives from his plate, and anticipated his breakfast with the ghosts of ancient Greece and Fallujah seated with him at the table. Yanna spoke to him as if he were one more beautiful phantasm who was passing through Athens under her watchful gaze.

* * *

Here's one more hyperreality. "All the Cars Honking Behind Us at the Gas Station." I am waiting to fill up a gas tank, or perhaps a request for two dollars or fifty cents, for gas was much cheaper back when I was twenty-five. After midnight the fish flies scatter over every surface, land in my hair, up my nose, bedazzled by the neon burning lights. I am the boy filling up the sports car tank, and the girl sitting in the bucket seat watches me. It is through her body that these words pass, through her eyes of a watchful girl, anticipating her boyfriend back from the candy machine and another drive through the black angry night, down by Lake Superior, its environs of marble waves moonlit by the universe in present tense.

* * *

"A Civil War Reenactor Walks into The Mason Jar" takes place in Cheney, Washington. The Mason Jar is a café where I was having coffee with a friend, Jonathan Johnson. In walks an actor dressed as a Confederate soldier. It was not hard to imagine his conversation on no work as an actor. He became a character in my poem: the last Confederate who opposed the Northern Army. There was a defiance in his costume, the manner in which he straddled the chair, drinking his bitter coffee and then asking for more. I gave him a cigarette too, and a bucket baby of a fast car he called Loreena. He was considering the Confederate dead at Cemetery Ridge. Perhaps he played Robert E. Lee. Through his sad eyes of hypertension he viewed the fallen soldiers who sacrificed everything for him.

* * *

I dreamed of Billy the Kid when we played outlaw with stick rifles. I didn't know when we set up croquet in my backyard that he once had played too. You might ask yourself what was Billy doing with a mallet in his hands that day the photographer caught him standing upright and contemplating his future. Maybe it was going to be in the next crack of a croquet ball rolling into cholla cactus. His future, I mean, one of killing twenty-two men in gunfights. He squared away to knock one of the Regulator's balls into the dust. He wore a top hat as if he were at a mad ball of the Englishman's ranch. He might have suspected that one day his father figure, John Tunstall, would be ambushed on the trail. Maybe in the croquet ball under his foot as he aimed the mallet down he foresaw that death. His buck teeth smiling into the sun, he wanted to be the fastest gun in the West. He heard the poetry of that mallet striking a spherical object like a heart. It was a photograph of him suspecting an approaching tragedy, wearing a top hat and a striped English shirt, in "The Last Photograph of Billy the Kid."

ACKNOWLEDGMENTS

The author wishes to acknowledge the following publishers of the poems in: *Dunes Review*: "Walt Whitman and His Lake Superior Baptism"; *Flyover Country*: "Dead River"; *The Glacier*: "Postcard from Paris," "Terminal," "Letters Jim Harrison May Never Read," "At Big Pink Where Bob Dylan Hangs His Hat Most of the Time," "On His Sixty-First Birthday One Could See Francisco Tadeo Isidoro Dancing in His Music Repair Shop," and "Miles Davis Playing on His Turntable"; *I-70 Review*: "At the Gilmore Drive-In Where James Dean Up on the Screen Lifted His Arms Slowly," "Philip Levine Dreams of Granada," and "His Canoe over the Watery Grave of Lake Superior"; *Oddball Magazine*: "John Lennon at the Old Marquette Inn"; *The Seventh Quarry*: "John Lennon Rows to Dorinish" and "Electric Mudman Moon"; *Slant: A Journal of Poetry*: "Baseball Had the Blood of Many on Its Cowhide," "Wildflowers," and "Teaching Poetry at the Prison on Thursday Nights"; *Speckled Trout River*: "Levon Helm Sings for All the Virgil Caines"; *this/that/lit*: "This Wheel on Fire"; and *Yooper Poetry: On Experiencing Michigan's Upper Peninsula*: "Beside the Breakwall near Five-Foot Splashing Waves."

* * *

David Dodd Lee selected six poems for *The Glacier*, Indiana University South Bend's online annual magazine, and through electronic conversations propelled these studies of character into poetry. A constant friend, his words helped shape this manuscript in subtle but powerful ways. Jonathan Johnson, in his redoubtable voice, made this a much stronger book, advising me on the shape of some poems. Ken Meisel was a spiritual guide who often left me breathless in his intense observations of erotic love. Cal Freeman rocked me each time with his heartfelt comments. Rodney Torreson was invaluable in every keen-eyed edit.

Dr. Ross Tangedal, extraordinary editor and muse to many poets, gave me the privilege of a second book—the sequel to all my noirish characters and rock stars who were essential to *And the Heart Will Not Quicken*. His book design and layout savvy were trusted endeavors and always beautiful to behold in the final copy. And thanks to press editorial director Brett Hill for his patience and professionalism.

Peter Markus knew exactly where to cut or move words around on a line. It was artful and genius. His honesty and deft scans made the poems stand out when they needed their own righteous recognition.

And the Heart Will Not Quicken came from the last line of William Everson's poem, "Fog."

Russell Thorburn is the author of several poetry collections, including *Let It Be Told in a Single Breath* (Cornerstone Press 2024). A National Endowment for the Arts recipient and first poet laureate of Michigan's Upper Peninsula, his poems have appeared in many literary journals and anthologies, including *North Dakota Quarterly*, *Dunes Review*, and *Sou'wester*. He lives in Marquette, Michigan, with his wife.

www.ingramcontent.com/pod-product-compliance
Lightning Source LLC
Chambersburg PA
CBHW031426120626
46545CB00006B/2293